Under the shadow of the Almighty

"in the Secret Place"

Under the shadow of the Almighty

"in the Secret Place"

Elizabeth Morgan

Dedicated

to my God-sent husband, Rev. Willie James Morgan, Jr.
Whose laughter is like sugar; it makes my life sweeter.
Without your loving concern, sustaining spirit, support, and
encouragement, this would not have been written.
You push me to be a better woman every single day.
I won't stop thanking you.
I love you to ~ infinity!

Under the Shadow of the Almighty

Copyright© 2020 by Elizabeth Morgan

Unless otherwise indicated, all Scripture quotations are taken from *The Holy Bible*, King James Version (KJV) English Standard Version (ESV)© 1987, 2001. All rights reserved.

Printed by IngramSpark, in the United States of America. One Ingram Blvd. La Vergne, TN 37086.

ISBN: 979-8-218-11156-4
Religion/Christian Living/General

Contents

Acknowledgments

Acknowledgment is given to my godmother, Mrs. Edna Milliner. I do not have enough words to express my gratitude to you. Thank you for keeping your promise to my mother.

Dr. Hurdis M. Bozeman, you have selflessly labored and invested your life in intercession for many years for leaders and people. I look to you as a prayer mentor and a spiritual mother. You are worthy of double honor! Thank you for imparting words of encouragement and prophesying Psalm 91. I will forever acknowledge your impartation of prayer in my life. You are and forever will be my *Inspiration*.

Dr. Israel Jones Sr., your entrepreneurial skills have endeared you to many hearts. You have taught me how to mentor and empathize with God's people through your ministry. This stance is the epitome of outstanding leadership. Thank you for your spiritual guidance and support.

Dorothy Benson and Charlotte Denise George-Reid, when we talk, I am reminded of what a true friend is no matter how long we are apart. Yes, we all have our differences, but that is what God used to bring us together. Ray Anthony Morris II, Bobby J. Sparks Jr., and Vernesia Gordon, you kept encouraging me to make these truths available. You all blew me away by seeing the potential in me by simply saying, *"Girl,* write the book!" My special cousin, Roneta Elmore, and our "need to talk" coffee times helped me grow so much. You've been there for me during the best, worst, and everything in between.

Finally, Dr. Naomi Caldwell and Dr. Kecia M. Ashley, thank you for your vision that has significantly influenced this book and my life. It challenged and encouraged me to delve more deeply into writing.

Foreword

It is a profound honor to have been asked to write a foreword to this powerful edition of *Under the Shadow*-a book that has an extraordinary testimony. About ten years ago, I was introduced to Evangelist Elizabeth Morgan on a trip to visit my parents. She served as the Lector, executive assistant to the pastor, and Sunday school teacher at my home church.

As I watched her working in excellence and serving in these capacities, her heart displayed a passion for pleasing God and giving Him glory. In that vein, I whispered to my mother, "Pray and look out for Elizabeth." I didn't know God would use her life to mend broken hearts.

Since then, I relocated back home and have seen her grow in her relationship with our Lord and Savior, Jesus Christ. It is a pleasure to know her in a genuine friendship that has advanced into a partnership in ministry.

First, Evangelist Morgan has a natural gift for reality. She takes the reader on her journey through chronic illness and the heartache of losing her parents, an extraordinary father and a phenomenal mother, without leaving you lost in her grief. She testifies over and over again of God's faithfulness. She can walk you through God's divine protection and love to become a triumphant Woman of God. I felt as though I sat down for a cup of coffee with her over the time it took me to read this book.

Second, Evangelist Morgan's writing and scripture references provoke the reader to reexamine what it truly means to be a true follower of Jesus Christ. Evangelist Morgan's dedication to God takes her to the place where her heart burns with the desire to go deeper and deeper into the knowledge of the beauty of the Lord.

Third, Evangelist Morgan truly embodies the spirit of Ruth in that she uses her beauty, intellect, humble spirit, and caring heart to uplift and she improves the lives of everyone she encounters. She listened to her spiritual mother as she guided and nurtured her prophetic spirit to meet her God-given husband, Reverend Willie James Morgan, Jr., as God designed Ruth for Boaz.

7

Evangelist Morgan has written a promising and healing book that will inspire and encourage women of all ages to stand in their truth. Finally, this is her first book, but it is an important book for you, for the church, and for those who are broken. *"Under the Shadow of the Almighty"* will take you on an emotional roller coaster ride. It will make you laugh, cry, and cheer for the heroine like you are at a championship football game. *"Under the Shadow of the Almighty"* is a beautiful testament to overcoming adversity through the power of forgiveness to embrace a brighter and prosperous future. And we know that all things work together for good to those who love God, to those who are called according to His purpose. (Romans 8:28 NKJV).

A life-changing and excellent read!

What Others Say About 'Under the Shadow'

I just finished reading/experiencing your life in *"Under the Shadow of the Almighty."* Wow!! Thank you. It was tremendous. What a testimony of faith and God's everlasting mercy and grace. Woman of God, I applaud the manifestation of His glory in your life. Thank you for not giving up or quitting because your example gives me the courage to run on and see what the peaceful end is. I know it's going to be a tool to help in the restoration of those who are suffering in silence. God bless your publication. I'm excited to see what Abba is going to do next.

-Naomi R. Caldwell, Ph.D.
Munsee/Lenape (American Indian)
Ramapough Lenape Nation
Providence, Rhode Island

Reading *'Under the Shadow'* is like talking to a friend whenever I move to a new chapter. Thank you so much for writing it! I couldn't put it down once I started reading. It is encouraging and challenging at the same time. All I can say is that it will touch everyone who reads it. It deals with many emotional and spiritual aspects of family, faith, grief, and walking in your calling. I am encouraging everyone to confess this Psalm.

-Ja'Nett Clark Agnew, M.Ed.
Tuscaloosa, Alabama

Under the Shadow has become one of my all-time favorites. Under the Shadow is a special book! A very good read and a look into her life. After reading it, I felt divinely inspired. It's an awesome book.

-Isong Idio Jr., CISP
Lagos, Nigeria

9

Introduction

We are living in perilous times. II Timothy 2, the Word says that in the last days, difficult times will come. In addition to the virus, we have seen huge earthquakes and how the earth triggered a tsunami. We have seen floods, tornados, fires, and civil unrest, not to mention deception, all at the same time. These events affected millions of people. If we ever needed a word from Heaven, it is now. For years, Psalm 91 has been my strength. It has made the difference between life and death in my life. It speaks prophetic, prolific poetry and promises us comfort and protection.

Although I have known about the psalms all my life, somehow, Psalm 91 spoke to my pain. Frantically, I was searching for answers on how to get my life together, and almost overnight, this one became my best friend. I was astounded by how accurately it reflected my pain.

On August 13, 2007, at 9:42 PM, I heard the Lord say, "Get your pen and write! Daughter, you will see things that you thought could not happen in your life. Promotion will come. You will be promoted in my kingdom, in my anointing, in my blessings, and your finances. I will anoint you for prosperity as you've never seen before. You will be one of the ones who will carry the load of spreading my word in these last days. The load will not be heavy because I will carry you. Many of your days will be hard but look up. I will bless you as never before, but you must walk in love with your brothers and sisters. Walk in love, faith, sowing, and reaping. Walk in the spirit of life. Yield to my spirit, beloved, and watch me do these things I have spoken to you."

Listen, if I never get another chance to tell you this, "the Lord is the conductor who arranges the affairs that are pronged to create the noise of stress in all of us." However, He will also bring us calm when our world seems chaotic. You will find refuge. God does not impose. He does not make you come to him for refuge, but He offers it anyway. If we learn to listen, we will hear the voice that calls each one of us. In addition, if we follow, we will find the secret place where the One who is love eternal dwells. There alone will we find strength and peace in His everlasting arms.

As the days of our Lord Jesus Christ draw near, these patterns of events will increase, and our cautious times will increasingly become more perilous. Perilous and dangerous, yes, but somehow through it all, God, by His Holy Spirit, will lead us through. In these difficult times, we should move every believer to love and support one another so we can overcome the tribulations of our days through Jesus Christ. Just as a virus naturally has spread, the same thing can happen spiritually.

To all of you end-time *warriors* and anyone who has experienced pain. The loss of a loved one, particularly those who are struggling now. I believe in the years ahead; Psalm 91 will be a major part of our vocabulary. Let us stay in prayer and ask God to purify our hearts and keep us from the enemy's deception in this hour so that we will be ready when He returns. If you are dwelling in God, you are dwelling in the One who is high above all things and above your troubles.

God has promised you that He will provide protectors. Your leaders are here to help extend that protection. Listen: Stop attacking your pastors! God called them to watch over you, and if you have not forgiven someone in the way you should, you are out of order. Honesty empowers. Love helps us grow. Will you draw near to God and let Him draw near to you?

One more thing! Many of you have suffered through pain silently, and you are wondering why a good God would let His child suffer. Yet the Lord has proven to you repeatedly through His abundance of grace that He has filled those hollow places with joy. You will survive and live to revive others. The truth is, we all have wounds. We all carry scars. But that is not the end of the story!

God has permitted me to write this book and to declare His divine protection. The woman of faith I am today is assured and bold, and my faith is much more expansive. The Spirit saw fit to allow this to come to pass. Each chapter is brief and can stand alone. This unique book has been a labor of love and compassion, and I hope these messages will change the readers' lives as they did in my life. I hope these pages will help inspire you to live a life that is pleasing to God.

There are somethings
You will only learn from God.

"Daughter, Write these words."
"A closer walk with Me is a life of continual newness.
As you focus your thoughts on Me, be aware that I am fully
attentive to you. I see you with a steady eye because
My attention span is infinite." Journal entry - June 26, 2004

My Defining Moment

In 2004 I met Dr. Hurdis M. Bozeman at Global Evangelical Christian College and Seminary. There was a quality in her life that I liked. I recognized that because I needed a mother when my mother died. She became my spiritual mother. As I learned how to communicate with her, I began changing because of this opportunity. This observation led to her encouraging me to write a book about my life to further inspire others. So I started writing. As quickly as I began to, I stopped. It was scary. I'm no writer. I'm an introvert. Shy and content. I enjoy being with people. But if I fail to embrace the limit of my introversion, I become tired, irritable, and ineffective. How was I to transform myself into an author? Let me tell it, essays and research papers were challenging enough, let alone a book. However, despite the late start, I set a goal. I was terrified, but I stayed committed. Writing is part of therapy for me. But, shockingly, somewhere along the way, I realized God had placed something in me that needed to come out.

On August 13, 2007, at 9:42 PM, I heard the Lord say, "Get your pen and write! Daughter, you will see things that you thought could not happen in your life. Promotion will come. You will be promoted in my kingdom, in my anointing, in my blessings, and in your finances. I will anoint you for prosperity as you've never seen before. You will be one of the ones who will carry the load of spreading my word in these last days. The load will not be heavy because I will carry you. Many of your days will be hard but look up. I will bless you as never before, but you must walk in love with your brothers and sisters. Walk in love, faith, sowing, and reaping. Walk in the spirit of life. Yield to my spirit, beloved, and watch me do these things I have spoken to you."

Fast-forward to 2019. I completed and published the first book titled "Walking with The King." An inspirational compilation outlining sermons and short stories derived from my mentor and pastor, Dr. Israel Jones, Sr. May I also conclude that not only did I have an obligation to write a book. The passion fueled me to do what I had never done before: to leave a realm of mediocrity.

I declare with a voice of triumph: "With men this is impossible, but with God all things are possible." (Matthew 19:26)

13

CHAPTER 1
It Takes A 'Village'

He who dwells in the secret place
of the Most High shall abide
under the shadow of the Almighty
(Psalm 91:1)

"When I imagine the warmth of a nest and the security of being under the wings of the nurturing love of a mother hen with chicks, it paints a vivid picture of the sheltering wing of God's protection that the psalmist refers to in this passage. God also gives you family to protect you. There is a difference between being on His wings and being under His wings."

Family means a lot to me. Not everyone has the same kind of family. It isn't important if your family isn't like mine or your best friend's because no matter who you call "family," they are all part of your own story. I was raised in a family in which aggressive shaming and verbal humiliation coexisted with lots of affection and care. I had difficulty embracing the term "dysfunctional." Since I felt and still feel attached to my siblings, I am proud of all the positive dimensions of our family life. I did not want to describe us using a term that implied our life together was all negative or destructive. I did not want my siblings to think I was disparaging them. I appreciate all the good things they have given to the family. However, with therapeutic help, I saw the term "dysfunctional" as a helpful description, not an absolute negative judgment.

On any day, I might have been given caring attention wherein my being an intelligent girl was affirmed and encouraged. In therapy, I pleasantly admitted that I felt genuinely loved by individual family members, especially my dad, mom, and grandfather. The experience of genuine love nurtured my wounded spirit and enabled me to survive. I am grateful to have been raised in a family that was caring. They gave what they had – *Love*. During the holidays, we gathered around, and everybody would tell the family stories. The house was throbbing, same as always: caramel and pound cakes, sweet potato pies, collard greens hissing in mom's pressure cooker, and everybody; and my mother, sister, brothers, wives, babies, aunts, cousins-talking too loud at the same time.

This story brings me to a time when I was around eight or nine and flooded with emotions about my mom's birth experience with me. The two of us were sitting at the kitchen table. Such a beautiful afternoon it was, with the sun shining through the windows and onto the clean floor, the trees resembling the Rocky Mountains in the distance. Everyone was telling stories of the past, laughing, and having fun with the time we shared with our family when I asked, "Mom, what was it like when I was born?" Mom's gestures were all familiar; the way she tilted her head and thrust out her lower lip when she had a thought, the way her eyes widened with childish glee when she had something interesting to talk about. I couldn't have asked God for a better day to hear her story.

15

Mom was about 5'4". She had honey-blonde hair color and a pixie haircut. She was confident in her beauty. Nice facial features with a beautiful smile. Her cheekbones were still high and strong, her skin smooth with brown skin tone. I called her a *classy lady*. She worked at the local hospital, and she could be demanding. She was very good at reading and writing, and she was creative. Her typical day involved getting us up early and ready for school, cooking, cleaning, and occasionally shopping. My mother was a good cook, and her specialty was baking cakes from scratch.

That day her happiness was tangible. As young as I was, I could feel it. She looked so happy and serene that it became a memory I stored in my mental photo album. One I could take out at will and enjoy. My radiant face was all she needed. Mom gave me a hopeful look. I could hardly sit still. As always, cheerful and casual, she kissed my cheek. I felt my shoulders tightening up like they invariably did during these conversations. I slid down in the chair. Closing my eyes, I allowed her to filter into my mind as she started her story. "Well, it was a difficult time," she said. Immediately I knew what she meant. She and my biological father were divorced before I came along. "What kind of difficult time, momma?" I asked. She thought for a moment.

"Your father and I are who we are. Accept it." She said.

"And what am I supposed to tell people about my parents?" I asked.

"Just tell the truth," Mom said. "That's simple enough."

My mother's name is Terry, and I know her family comes from a well-known community living in the central area. I don't know much about my father's family, but I believe most of them worked as farmers. My mother tried to describe my father's family to me, but I couldn't visualize them. I knew they had seen me as a baby, but I had no recollection. Holding onto my hand, she whispered, the real story went like this: "You know, Toni baby, the days of you being a tiny baby were the happiest times of my life. I remember it as though it was yesterday. When you were born, I sat in bed feeling so proud at thirty-six that I produced you. You were a small, perfect little person. I felt so much love and tenderness for you. I wanted to hold you. I tried to look after and protect you. I wanted a good life for you.

That's what I felt. When I found out I was expecting my eighth child, I knew it would be different this time. During those times, a doctor practiced, but he moved away. However, there was a midwife in the area named Ms. Elizabeth Foster. Towards the beginning of my delivery, I was completely confined to bed and dependent on her for everything. I was impressed with how much time she spent getting to know me. As time went on, we became more comfortable at my home. My labor started late the night before with back pain that kept coming and going throughout the night and the following day. I took walks to keep my mind off the contractions, but I felt you move less than what I felt was normal. I was in labor for 19 hours! The labor progressed rapidly, and Ms. Foster asked if she could break my water, and I agreed.

You entered on Thursday, August 4th at 9:04 P.M., 7lbs, 4oz. I pushed for forty minutes when she pressed down on my abdomen and asked me to push. I was shocked when she placed you on my belly and so excited! You came with the loudest cry of at least five minutes. I named you after Ms. Elizabeth Foster because she showed me love. She spoke words of comfort to me as she swaddled you. "God said, be not afraid. I will use your baby in these end times. I have a shield of protection around her. I have My hands on her; she is my eye's apple. There will be people who will try to come against her, but they should be careful. I have chosen her and will send the right people into her life to guide her where she needs to be. 'I Am' will be with her."

As mom finished telling me her story, she looked at me, and I guess she thought about the words. She placed her hand on my forehead and prayed: "God, I thank you! I ask you to watch over every word spoken over my child's life. Protect and shield her as you have promised." In Jesus' Name! I believe God allowed Ms. Foster to speak into my mother's life to save her. I am still here. Glory to God! Remember Anna? She was a prophetess and the daughter of Phanuel of the tribe of Asher. (Luke 2:36). I also believe Ms. Foster was mom's Anna! Mom's story is a beautiful picture of utter dependence on God. It's a beautiful example of how God provides for us and a beautiful illustration of trusting him. Mom experienced a difficult marriage, financial worries, and unfulfilled longings.

I'm sure there were days my mom barely survived, struggled to make it through, and even wondered if life was worth it. As a kid, I had no idea of everything my mother kept away from me. She never put me in "harm's way!" She was the ultimate protector. Now that I am an adult, I still don't understand all she went through, and it's mind-blowing. Some things I understood later on. Therefore, I'm glad she wasn't weak, and I am grateful that she gave me what I couldn't get from anyone else. Although things were far from ideal at birth and throughout childhood, she loved me and spoke destiny into my life!

Will you do me a favor? Take your mouth off of God's anointed! And take notice of what flies out of your mouth. Every word you speak with faith will change things for good or bad. That is why it is essential to say what God's Word says. If you say negative things that go against God's Word, you bring negative, evil things into your life. The worst thing that can happen is for something to come out of your mouth that brings death. Cursing gives God nothing to work with. You and I are where we are because of the words we spoke yesterday, the day before, and so on. What comes out of your mouth is firing either Satan's or God's weapon. Because He can do what He said He would do. God's word is right. He will make a liar out of everyone that speaks against you. I've said it before, and I will repeat it. Let God be true and every man a liar.

Some said I would never amount to anything. That devil is a lie! The Word of God says, if any man is in Christ, he is a new creature; old things have passed away, and all things have become new (2 Corinthians 5:17). He is not finished with you yet. He is still presenting you as His righteous people. He will not schedule your next appointment until you are mature enough to handle what He has for you. Our times are in His hands. So many times, as Christians, we mentally agree that the Lord is our refuge, but that is not enough. Did you know that your words are powerful? Power is released in saying it out loud. When we say it and mean it, we are placing ourselves in His shelter. By voicing His Lordship and His protection, we open the door to the secret place. I grew up watching mom handle all kinds of obstacles life threw at her. I'm sure she cried herself to sleep many nights, but she still got up every morning and did an amazing job raising us.

I could never be weak. I learned from the best. She raised us in a Christian home, and we went to church every Sunday. I never heard her using profanity, and she raised us to do the same. She didn't seem to have a worry in the world, and most importantly, she didn't care what other people thought. God controlled my mother's happiness. How many of you believe that God will send someone to reassure you that He is with you when you think your life is over?

The Blessing of Two in One

The pieces of my life I've always known about are enough to make me whole. I'm happy knowing where I came from, but I realize I'm blessed to have my biological and extended family. As I mentioned earlier, family means a lot to me. Relationships matter because we are all woven together into a story. We should not neglect the things that hold us together. Blessings are holy and cannot be corrupt because they come to us from our Father. The blessing of God transforms all that is visible and tangible in our lives. These blessings are meant to be shared interchangeably. We are blessed to be a blessing to one another. The blessing is when God favors your life in ways that change the enemy's narrative to work on your behalf toward your growth and benefit. That's Love. And the truth of the matter is: you can never lose what you have given in truth.

Not only did my mother have unlimited time to share with me her life experiences, but she also loved taking me to see my God-parents, Edna and James. We met when I was hospitalized as a child with an acute vaso-occlusive crisis. She and my mom worked until retirement in the inpatient unit. Their adoption of me as one of their own also changed the trajectory of my life. Godparents confer blessings and the fullness of life. Much like my mom, Edna is a breath of fresh air. She has brilliant intellect, wisdom, and the patience of Job. Maybe she is generous to a fault, but she is caring.

Her compassion is beyond measure. When I think about it, families just don't get together like we used to. One of my fondest memories is our visit to Thanksgiving. Back in the good old days, that was the tradition. Everybody went to grandma's house until she could no longer take care of business. My godparents lived in the next city over. I always thought they lived in another state. It took us so long to get there. I remember a couple of times mom had missed the road to turn on, and we drove what seemed like hours.

I tried counting the number of times I could sing "Over the river and through the woods," but I always lost count and fell asleep. It was an hour-and-a-half ride, so I'm sure everyone was tickled pink when I fell asleep. But! I am sure they were still humming that catchy tune when we arrived. The smell of southern food lingered on the porch as we entered the house. Everybody is talking loud and at the same time. Did I mention that they were a big family, five boys and one girl? Can you imagine being out-numbered on both sides of my family? I loved seeing momma Edna pouring the last bit of cake mixture into the pan because I would be rewarded with the bowl. I used my fingers to slide around its creamy, buttery mixture, and at the last taste, my god-sister would laugh and say, "it's just dough!"

Perhaps it's no surprise that my god-parents would always send me Christmas presents, a doll or a book. Normally, they would send a card a few days before my birthday. It was always something funny, never anything sappy. Mama Edna's love language is giving. She gives without worrying that she has enough for herself. I'll admit, at times, I think she is too generous. I noticed that she had collected people, adding to her life's mission the care of anyone who can benefit from extra motherly love and attention. The way she cared for folks inspired me to follow her lead. From my godfather, I learned even more. He was endowed with a special grace that made him tower above other men. He was warm and steadfast, a man whose principles would not bend, and he had within him a rare strength that sustained not only me and all the family but all those who sought his advice and leaned upon his wisdom. My godfather passed in 2003, just two days before my 31st birthday. He was supposed to be a part of that celebration.

The memory of losing him didn't disappear in a consistent and irrevocable reverse chronological manner. It retreated like waves at low tide, always around my birthday. It would recede and then return, but not quite to the same point, it had been before. It can be sad for those who have lost their fathers or father figures. While it may get easier with time, grief isn't linear. Some days will be harder than others, and some years better than not. But the days passing don't have to be a total loss (unless, of course, that's what you need to heal).

I use Father's Day to remember how strong and faithful to God, my godfather was. I try to remember that he is always with me in my heart. To this day, Mama Edna checks in often to see how we are doing. She continues to teach me the value and importance of family. And it is a blessing for me that I have Two in One.

The Brothers

Growing up with five brothers was fun, but sometimes I wished they were girls. Do not get me wrong! I love my brothers, but my mom, sister, niece, and I were always out numbered. Can you imagine how often we went into the bathroom and the toilet seat was up? I never understood why I had so many brothers. Reflecting back, I can see how I had no choice but to be nice to my siblings because I learned that pleased God. Never having to take sides with anyone was favorable for me.

One altruistic memory of my two younger brothers is when they invented a chopper on wheels out of used bicycle parts. Fish-tailed them in the streets and raced with the other boys to the ball diamond (our neighborhood park). They were a rowdy bunch, building go-carts and then crashing them into trees and blowing up their fingers with firecrackers. Like all boys, they both seemed intolerably cruel to me and got away with anything as far as I was concerned.

Growing up with them was a challenge for me. However, I always thought my youngest was the natural leader because he was our quietest. He was the creative one as well, especially with electronics. I still think he was the one who made the boom box that caught on fire. The other is outspoken and the most adventurous one in the family. He was intrigued by birds.

As an adult, I have not figured out how he threw a rock from a great distance and hit a bird. That is a story on its own. He also had a love for wrestling. If a fight broke out on the school bus or in the neighborhood, he was usually the one who started it. It did not matter to him. Somehow, his opponent always ended with a bite mark on the chest, ear, or arm. After so many fights ending like this, everyone concluded that maybe it was his brand.

As if to say, "remember who put that there." Now you know who the fighter is in the family. Don't laugh! Every family has one. That's why I always wanted to tag along with him. He had learned early to look and act tough, especially with the other older boys he hung around with. "No, girl. You can't go. You be crampin' my style," He replied. "I don't care. I'm going anyway. Besides, Momma said you gotta watch me today," I said, knowing that when my momma said something, she meant business. He knew better than to disobey mom. She did her best to keep us in line and had been known to use both broom and belt on them when they broke the rules. I knew my brother hated for me to tag along with him.

He was much older and had his own set of friends from the neighborhood. "Well, just keep your mouth shut, and don't do anything stupid," He warned." "Me and my boys got some business to take care of." He swaggered a little, making sure I noticed. I grinned and ran quickly to join them on the street. He and his friends like to pretend to be tough, but not all of it is pretending.

We learned early in the area around our streets that walking with an air of being in control was often necessary for survival. "You hear Oil-base got beat up last night?" my brother asked his friend as they walked down the street. "Yeah, man, he had it comin' to him. You don't take the money and not get tightened up. He's lucky he ain't dead." I was listening carefully, saying nothing, but taking it all in-confident. Although my stomach tightened with a mixture of fear, I didn't let my brother know. I could handle the knowledge of activities of boys much older than me. I didn't think it was unusual to discuss fights, drug deals, and muggings. That's how the world functions around me. There was no alternative to compare it to. They continued to walk down the street that summer afternoon, laughing, cursing, and spitting just to show this little bit of turf belonged to them. They had no particular destination and ended up in a small, grassy spot not far from the abandoned house.

My Sister is in Charge

During my childhood, I saw my sister as the authoritative figure in almost everything. She was a good-hearted person. Strong-willed, supportive, understanding, and independent, as well as loving. She resembled our mom a lot. Some people often mistook her for mom. She also had one child, my niece. My sister was a stern disciplinarian. She was mature enough to take on this task while trying to keep up with her problems. In age, my sister and I were twenty-five years apart. Being the oldest child, I am sure, had its rewards for her; you can imagine we were as different as the sun and moon. We never had that special sisterly bond I longed for, the kind where you could share your inner feelings. Our age differences never led to arguments over privacy except for the days I went a little too far snooping in her perfume and playing dress up. I had many positive and negative experiences with my sister. For instance, I hated getting my hair combed, especially with braids. I was a tomboy, and I had to see what everybody was doing, and she was cutting into my playtime. It felt like traction as she snatched and pulled for hours of braiding. When she called my name, my niece ran out the door as fast as she could to ride her bike; as I stood there brooding while my sister was yelling, "Come on, 'Lil' brat!" "Why do you always have to call me first?" I asked. "Because I can, and you will be glad I did when I'm finished." She said.

People have often said that facial expressions reveal a lot about a person. I had this 'thing' I did with my eyes when I was aggravated. Yes, I rolled them! I didn't think she would notice, but she did and popped me on my forehead with the back of the comb. Seemly, that pop went straight to my soul. That hurt! You'll, that's not funny.

She was the first multitasker I had ever seen. She could comb hair, make Kool-Aid, and cook (chicken, collard greens, corn on the cob, potato salad, cornbread, baked peach crumble pie). While watching her favorite daytime soap operas (General Hospital, Guiding Light, and One Life to Live), *Y'all remember!*

My First Best Friend

As my sister finished with the last braid, my niece came screaming, "Toni, Toni!" from the back door; to tell me that her bicycle was fixed. Somehow, I missed how she got out of getting her hair braided. But she insisted we go ride our bikes, and I gave in to her wishes and decided to take her up on it. It was refreshing.

Riding our bikes was our favorite thing to do together. My niece is six months older than I am. Our relationship was like no other. We became special solely because, having grown up in a house with boys, I needed someone to listen to my daily life experiences.

She knew everything and wasn't afraid of doing dumb stuff, either. On this hot summer day, as we sat on our little front stoop, trying to cool off from riding our bikes in the heat of the day, we looked around at our neighborhood and sighed, thinking of something to do. Our thoughts and eyes were on the cold Kool-Aid.

We knew my sister did not like to be disturbed while watching her soaps, but we were just thirsty kids on a hot day that needed a quick and easy cool-down. We also knew we couldn't have any before dinner. Instead of asking for a cup, we were trying to figure out a way to get it. We never thought about the consequences and never considered that our stealing could get us in deep trouble. As my niece was on the lookout, I eased into the kitchen to grab the biggest cup I could find so we could share. As soon as I opened the refrigerator, my sister heard me and yelled, "Get out of that refrigerator, girl! And don't even think about getting any Kool-Aid!" I knew she could see through that wall. In our defense, I asked, "but we're thirsty. May we have something to drink?" "Drink some water." She said. My niece cut me a wicked look and started laughing. You all know what I did. Yes. I rolled my eyes and slammed the refrigerator. She yelled, "Slam it again, *heifer!*"

Unsuccessful at the Kool-Aid, we decided to go see the candy lady. My niece's favorite was the giant Sweet-Tart candies she licked until her tongue was so raw. I loved chocolate, but it was gone too quickly. Hence, I usually got a Sugar Daddy, which lasted practically half the day and always had a funny poem printed in pink letters on the stick like: *"To keep your feet from falling asleep, wear loud socks they can't be beaten."*

The bond that she shared with me is that of otherhood. We had little disagreements, but none of that caused us to fight until one of us could not get our way. We both communicated differently. We did not match each other because our personalities and habits were too distinguished, but I did not care about it. I thought it was only my personal feelings. Naturally, she was a stubborn girl, and it took her a long time to realize her mistakes. She was once punished for being stubborn. After all, she was only child. In addition to listening to music, sharing a room, our clothes, and food, we shared who we were. Whenever I needed moral support when I was scolded for doing something wrong, I would run toward her. I admired how she kept my little secrets, sat with me, and did my homework, even though it was wrong.

Sometimes we would share our dreams, hopes, and fears with a few prayers at bedtime, but these things changed with a significant emotional withdrawal. The day came that she would soon be leaving. It was her dream come true! My sister had been looking for a job for some time, and they would be moving to New Jersey. My mom's two brothers and mother, Mittie, were there.

Therefore, my mom decided that my sister couldn't decline this opportunity. It would offer her a better quality of life, and they deserved that. Ultimately, this would be the best decision for her family, but selfishly, I wanted them to stay. We would miss birthdays, sleepovers, and picnics in the backyard. What would I do with my time? Who will I do all of our favorite activities with? Will I do them alone? Will I ever find another friend like her? The one person who was such an enormous part of my day-to-day life was suddenly going to be limited to phone calls. It would take some time to navigate without her.

As for my sister, I felt like it would be the last time we were going to see each other, and somehow we both knew each other knew. Of course, neither of us said anything, but it did make a difference. Our conversation was less flippant and more direct, but she hugged and kissed me goodbye between our bursts of talking. Of course, when they left, I felt alone. I completely shut down. The only person who would give me the time of day to talk and listen to what I had to say was gone. It felt like a strong whirlwind had come, and I stopped breathing. No wonder God is the restorer of our souls and loves us, but my heart ached. I cried for a long time.

Every day I would mention to my mom how much I missed her. Saying goodbye is hard. "Toni baby, I know you will miss her, but also have hope that they both find happiness in their new home," Mom said. This move served as a loss for me. The one person who surrounded me with her crazy laughter, witty jokes, and protective instincts has left me. How could someone so close and dear to me leave? Why was I feeling so much pain? I was a child, but I was heartbroken. Thanksgiving and Christmas would come and go so fast. The months flew by in a blur. Once in a while, the phone would ring. My mother would answer it. "Just a minute," she'd say.

Then in a whispered voice, "Toni baby, come get the phone. It's your niece." We talked briefly, mostly about her new friends and how she's adapting to her new school. I could hear the excitement in her voice when we spoke. She even had a northern accent. My silent words were more introspective than prayer. She shifted the

25

conversation, "Pray for me, will you?" she asked. "Of course I will." She said that every night before we went to sleep. After that, the calls grew less. It seems we have little control over what sticks and what doesn't. That's the way memories are. I feel there was a loss to what a friendship was destined to be because she was the first to be my First Best Friend.

"The Village"

The summer of 1981 was extraordinary in every possible respect. This particular summer, throngs of my relatives, children, and friends loved to gather at my cousin David's house. His mom (Aunt Ruth) and my mom were sisters. David stood about five feet seven, but people often thought he was much taller. A largeness about him expressed itself in the quality of his thought and the size of his ambitions. At fifty-five, David was self-employed. He was typically too practical to pay careful attention to his appearance. He had his own small carpentry business, wood-framing, and much more. He was a jack of all trades. To me, he could do everything. I loved his faith. His magnetic charm was indisputable. By contrast, David was a bona fide math scholar.

I never knew he could dissect numbers in his head the way he had. I loved talking with him, asking questions, and pointing out objects he could calculate on a whim. Also, during this time, I observed that David was recovering from a severe foot sprain and his injury made him passive at times. His wife was attuned to his moods and was conscious of his pain. I also sensed his aloofness. That evening, he waved when he saw me. He was chilling in his hammock after a long day's work.

We never understood how he could lay there and let the sun beam on his face. "Hey, Tone Tone!" he called out. I hugged him and kissed his cheek. He wore a bulky gray shirt with light stains and black leather boots. His cup was half filled with his favorite libation in his hand. He emptied his tobacco ashes into a wooden tray. He had washed his hands, but his neck and face were still sweaty and dark with grime, but I didn't mind.

After that, one of my cousins pushed me to ask him for a dollar to get ice cream. We knew the ice cream truck would always come around the same time every day, and we looked forward to the treats. Then, our whole mood changed. I knew I did not need to move any further. I was fine where I was. Fear gripped my soul. Listen, just because you are anointed doesn't mean you will not have anxiety. I was nervous! He started mumbling when he heard the music chimes. He jumped up from his hammock and started walking towards us. "Damn it, I can't get no sleep!" He said.

I sensed my smallness of myself in comparison to my cousins ahead of me. It was then I saw the black figure retrieved from his pocket. As he got closer, he held his pistol in the air and fired twice. Everybody ran in different directions, looking to see where the shots came from. The driver immediately put his truck in reverse and backed backward to the entrance of the community, leaving a huge cloud of black smoke spinning from the tires as he drove off.

Cousin David said he was not going to shoot the man. He just wanted to scare him because he interrupted his nap. He said, "Hell, you'll meet at somebody else's house tomorrow 'cause I ain't coming home, and don't ask me no questions!" He looked at me and said, "You started asking for a damn dollar." He ended up buying ice cream for everyone. My family will always remember this, and we still laugh about this memory often.

All of the families who lived around here were tight on cash. Some were tighter than others, but all of us kids were scrawny and wore faded shorts, raggedy shirts, and sneakers with holes or no shoes. None of us kids got allowances. When we wanted money, we walked along the roadside, picking up beer cans and bottles we redeemed for two cents each. If a fight broke out while we were playing, our neighborhood bodyguards would break it up. Nobody got hurt; we were all family. Unfortunately, there was a lot of negative peer pressure in my neighborhood, so much so that it became the norm to do the wrong thing instead of the right thing. It was what your peers expected of you. If you didn't conform, you might be labeled "not cool." It was difficult for me to pick friends. I didn't fit in with those around me. I did many things my gut told me I shouldn't do. Things I didn't want to do. Not only was it hard, but it was continuous. Every day offered options to give up or give in.

Don't get me wrong; we made lots of mistakes. We often made foolish decisions and frequently suffered the consequences of impulsive behavior. We weren't bad kids, but just kids needing focus and direction. What was most important to us was who ran the fastest. The only rule was to come home when the streetlights went on. Many other kids lived in our neighborhood, and we all played together after school. We also played red-light- green-light, tag, football, Red Rover, or nameless games that involved running hard, keeping up with the pack, and not crying if you fell.

Mom was not one of those fussy mothers who got upset when you came home dirty, played in the mud, or fell and cut yourself. She said people should get things like that out of their systems when they were young. Once, an old nail ripped my thigh while I was climbing over a fence at my friend Tracy's house. Tracy's mother thought I should go to the hospital for stitches and a tetanus shot. "Nothing but a minor flesh wound," Mom declared after studying the deep gash. "People these days run to the hospital every time they skin their knees," she added. With that, she sent me back out to play. I mentally blocked out this summer that my sister and niece were no longer around, but I still had my moments. Images drifted through my mind of my niece making us breakfast. The eggs were rubbery, the toast like cardboard. It felt good to remember those things, but I dried my cheeks with my hands.

Spend as much time as you possibly can with your family. In doing so, you will find your purpose in relationships. Make it part of your life plan to explore the things that ignite you into becoming a better person. When you treat people right and do good things for your family or, for that matter, other people, it affects not just them but also those around them. Memories of my childhood come back and are so clear and vivid it's like being young again. Sadly, as we grow older, those moments of wonder become rare.

It's funny now because growing up, I only thought about how I would make it out of there. In the old cliché: You can pick your friends, not your family. Knowing all this, I resolved to be content with what I had. During the rest of that summer, I did my best to be or at least seem to be optimistic, and I prayed that God would keep us all together. I can say it takes the love of a 'village' to raise a child. Yes, Crenshaw Village! Much Love.

CHAPTER 2

He Knows Us

I will say of the Lord,
He is my refuge and my fortress:
my God; in him will I trust.
(Psalm 91[2])

"You cannot get away from his presence.
To realize that God knows me; knows where I am, and where
I'm going, and what I'm doing, and that he even knows
what I'm thinking may seem a little ominous to us.

29

Growing up, I was timid. My internal fears seemed to lessen because I have a family who loves me, but things were becoming clearer to me that if I wanted to fill the void of not fitting in with the crowd, I needed to start reading and studying the Word of God. This alone time was great for me. It served as a mere breakthrough. The Bible is clear: God created us for His glory. He knows us more intimately than anyone else in this life. God sorts out all the details of our lives. For instance, the baby's heart is pumping blood at week four. God is there perfectly working as He desires to work. Throughout the pregnancy, God forms the child's inward parts: kidneys, liver, heart, appendix, and blood vessels. They are all perfectly put together while in the darkness of the mother's womb.

No matter the circumstances surrounding your conception, ethnicity, or gender, your existence is intentional. You are not a mistake. God, after all, doesn't make mistakes. He is never surprised, never amazed. He never wonders about anything, nor does He seek information or ask questions. He doesn't miss a thing. He knows when you are going through a difficult time. He knows what we need before we need it. He knows us better than the FBI knows us. He knows more information about your Google searches than Google. He knows the heart behind it. He knows more than the CIA or Homeland Security about national threats to our country. He knows more than the IRS about your finances. He knows and sees everything about each of us. You can't sin and get away with it. Now, you can hide from your Pastor-Others-Family, but GOD SEES IT! There is nowhere you will ever go that is outside His sight and presence. He knows everything in an eternal now. He does not have to look back to remember, nor does He need to project into the future in some hypothesis.

With all of the knowledge we have in books, hard disks, servers, or the internet "cloud," God knows and always has known. He knows more than the professors; Einstein and Newton are simpletons. I said all this to say; even when we try to run from Him-He is there. I think it gets to the very core of what we all need and what we all long for. To be known and yet loved. Having been known in a way that someone is fully aware of us in the most intimate of details; our faults, our past, our idiosyncrasies, and yet still loves us. Here's something else God knows: He knows all your

30

goodness and your acts of kindness and will not let them pass without a response! Now sometimes, maybe frequently, you get discouraged. You've reached out. You've given. You've gone without mentioning it. You've achieved and got it done. But in all this, no one seems to have noticed or appreciated you. Nobody says anything. Others just compete with you all the more. And it crushes your spirit. You don't feel like contributing or even playing hard or trying. Every time you helped someone unkind to you. Every time you let others go first. God celebrates all that is good.

Almighty God knows all these, and they are treasures in heaven. God knows what is best for us. He knows what is truly good. And you know what? So many times, we are doing everything we can to protect ourselves, even when it comes down to eating healthy food, obeying safety rules, and even going to a doctor when we need to. God is pleased when we do wise things. He is the only one who can protect us from the problem. Do you know why God calls us His sheep? It's because a sheep is the only animal with no protection. When I fear something bad will happen, I say, "Jesus, you are my Shepherd, and I am your sheep." Any time we look at the attributes of God, it should evoke praise. His perfections should leave us in astonishment. But there's more.

Tucked away in Psalm 91 is an invitation to trust God. If we ask what the burden of this passage is, I will sum it up like this: for us to know the God who knows us. The key word in this is the word "know." Well, what else does God know? He knows every word on our tongue. Did you notice that God says you are supposed to say out loud that God is your place of safety and protection? He wants you to tell Him that you trust Him.

It is enough to just think about God. When you say God's Word out loud and believe it-something happens in the spiritual realm. It is easy to see why God likes for us to say it out loud to Him. How would someone feel if they lived in the house with their mother and father and saw them every day, but they never said anything out loud to them? That wouldn't feel very good, would it? When you tell God that you believe Him when He says, He will protect you, God hears it. His angels hear it, and the devil also hears it.

Then God can say, "Devil, you cannot hurt him. He believes My Word, and he is protected," and God's angels work to protect you as well. How can it be that God knows our very thoughts and words? David says in Psalm 139:13-16 "For you formed my inward parts; you knitted me together in my mother's womb. I praise you, for I am fearfully and wonderfully made. Like a cloth on a loom, God has fashioned every one of us. The fact of the matter is, if you have been around the church for a while, you probably do not live like you believe this statement, but if you are new to the church or new to Christianity, this might come off as a cliché. However, it should comfort us. It should bring peace to us, but do you know what it does to most people? It scares them!

I was eight years old when I was born again, attending a summer revival meeting one night with my mom at our church. Sometimes, I would sneak away and have bible study alone to receive salvation. Thank God, He understands the child in us. The gospel treasure within us lends purpose and grit to our lives. He must have known the burning desire He placed in my heart. Although that is glorious, my first meeting with Jesus was simply the doorway to a life filled with promises. I heard His voice, felt His love, embraced His protection, and became like Him through the working of His in-dwelling spirit. I have come to tell you that we all can have a testimony every day of experiencing God's supernatural work in and around us. I am positive you can think of something that represents security to you personally.

God knows our needs and cares for us. In many people, this thought of God knowing and seeing everything they do or think can produce fear. That fear is manifested in an attempt to run from God. With God, we have no privacy. He is everywhere we go. You might want to run from the presence of God, but you can't. There is no ladder you can climb that will take you high enough to get out of the view of God. No airplane will take you high enough. A trip to space takes you not closer or further away from the presence of God.

In the same way, you can't dig a hole deep enough to get out of the vision of God. God knows your name. You belong to Him. And you are called by name and invited to come and take your place at the table. You are invited to feast upon God's abundant and everlasting love for you. May you satisfy your greatest hunger and thirst and be inspired to share the good news.

A little side note. In my jewelry box rests a necklace that I seldom wear. It is sentimental. I could never come to part with it because it belonged to my grandmother, who gave it to me as a child. I love it, but the color has faded. A couple of the gems are missing, the clasp has broken, and I should have thrown it away by now. I have no use for it, and I do not think I will ever wear it again. Logic says; I should throw it out and use that space for something else. That is what logic says. The necklace has a sign that says, "Made in America," so it could not be replaced. This particular necklace is unique. To me, it is one of a kind.

Even though the necklace has lost its shine, it has not lost its value. It is still valuable in my sight, not because of its function, but because of its maker. Does this make sense to you? Think of it like this. You and I are different. There is only one you and one me. We were not put together on an assembly line. We are not an accident. We are specifically gifted and positioned on this earth by the master builder-the chief cornerstone. Nevertheless, as kingdom people, we have a value that is so rare because of whose we are, not because of what we can do. We belong in a kingdom where we are granted membership. Yes! We are adopted into God's kingdom.

We do not earn it. We have to accept it. Because of that, we serve God, not man. And so, as God protects us, we will have those moments where life gets complicated, and the pain will often be hard for you to handle, but just when you think you cannot handle it anymore, look up! He is your fortress! God told Satan that you can touch his stuff but can't touch his soul. Hallelujah!

What are you going to do while you are going through this chapter of your life? Just like Job said, the Lord giveth, and the Lord taketh away; but still blessed be the name of the Lord (Job 1:21). No one person needs more of the blood of Jesus than any other. We are not the folk who don't know God. People who do their own thing all week and then run into the Lord's house on Sunday and get all pious and self-righteous, you know, the ones who do everything.

Even in the midst of this, I am reminded of what Paul tells us in 2 Timothy 2:19; nevertheless, the foundation of God stands sure, having this seal, God knows them that are His. Jesus died once and for all. He formed us in the womb. He knows our frame. He fashions our days. He knows our thoughts. He hears our words.

He knows when we sit down and when we stand up. He protects us. His hand is upon us. He who inhabits all things is near to us. We cannot escape His presence. In the light, He sees us. In the dark, He sees us. He searches us. He changes us. Here is true intimacy. I John 1:7, "But if we walk in the light, as He is in the light, we have fellowship one with another, and the blood of Jesus Christ His Son cleans us from all sins. If I can help show you more of God, it will be only through what He has said in His Word. It will not be by ingenuity but faithfulness. This psalm tells us to speak life! God's Word is your weapon. Oh, how deeply He Knows Us.

CHAPTER 3

The Only Safe Place

*Surely he shall deliver thee
from the snare of the fowler and the
noisome pestilence.
(Psalm 91[3])*

"Without a doubt," the psalmist declares,
"God will deliver you.

This verse speaks about the enemy that sneaks up on you, unseen. They come with wicked and deadly intents. Like the fowler, the deadly pestilence comes by stealth to destroy. It is a microscopic disease that comes from nowhere and inflicts deadly harm upon those it seizes. Whether they come by night or day, the one who trusts the Lord does not need to fear. When God is on your side, there is no need to fear the sudden, unexpected attack of the enemy. It took me a while to see the spiritual side of the enemy attacks and the internal workings of warfare in the body as a parallel concept with the disease.

There are all kinds of enemies: temptations, spiritual enemies, and physical enemies. Train yourself to stop during the split second when temptation rears its ugly head. "If God wants us to walk in health, why did He create germs?" God put this preventive promise in verse 3 for you and me to stand on for protection from both ways harm can destroy a life. Now the setting of this Psalm is interesting because we don't know what it is. We know that the Psalmist describes the ongoing sovereign protection of God's people and that God is ever protecting them in all dangers and terrors that surround them daily.

Say aloud: "God deliver me from the snare of the trapper; that thing that makes me lose my temper, that lust that tries to rise in my heart, that person who constantly offends me, that critical word that comes flying out of my mouth in a heated moment and that situation that always causes me to get frustrated." Like you, I always thought a pestilence attacked crops, bugs, locusts, grasshoppers, spider mites, mildew, or root rot. However, to my surprise, I found that pestilence attacks people, not crops! Pestilence is "any virulent or fatal disease; an epidemic that hits the masses of people." These deadly diseases attach themselves to a person's body with the intent to destroy it. But God tells us in verse 3 that He will deliver us from these deadly diseases.

Deadly Snare

Sometimes the traps of the enemy are physical traps sent to destroy you. My childhood memories reflect good and bad times, but every moment makes my life precious. However, a sad memory always resonates within my heart stronger, and a good memory makes me feel positive, yet a bad one has the power to help me grow up and understand what is important in my life.

One sad memory I recall. I felt horrible with a bad headache. It seemed like a migraine. Although I didn't have a fever, I felt horrible. I started throwing up that night and continued through the next day. I rested as best as I could but was still in pain. The next day I wasn't getting any better, so my mom took me to the doctor, who prescribed antibiotics. Later that day, they saw where I had spots around my neck and belly. It turned out to be measles! At this point, I had managed to eat and drink a bit. But the last day was retching. They finally took me back to the doctor and immediately sent us to the local hospital. They saw it was getting harder for me to breathe, and I was struggling for air. The hospital gave me oxygen and x-rayed my chest.

That's when they discovered I had a bad case of pneumonia, and the test revealed that I was severely anemic. When we got home from the hospital, I was treated like a little princess, with extra privileges and freedom from chores. I always remained a feeble-looking child. They kept nurturing and nurturing, yet I remained physically weak. People have no idea what you go through every day. There is no way to predict how a thing will affect your child or you as an adult. Complications can happen. It was a contagious disease that could have taken me out of this world. The unseen subatomic, bacterial-like dangers infiltrate systems that are not obvious or seen with the naked eye. A perilous pestilence!

We are enrolling through dangers that hang over us and are unknown until they affect us. It is odd how our earliest memory in life comes back to us again and again. Yet, even in the uncertain moments of dangers seen and unseen, God's promise of comfort is that He will deliver. He will go ahead of the believer and ensure they will be cared for beyond what they see and even what they do not see.

Once it becomes fixed in our minds, it forms a symbol we draw from for the rest of our days. Though no one could have known it at the time, my life would never again be the same. Yet, for nearly all my life, I felt as though loneliness was an enemy on assignment against me and that I had to master it to be of any consequence.

During these years, I witnessed the holiness that would later define my life. One evening I walked into my mother's bedroom and found her on her knees, her Bible before her, praying aloud. I thought it was amazing and asked her about it. She told me that she reads the Bible every evening at seven o'clock and then knelt in prayer. It had been her habit for years. Though I cannot explain it, I immediately sensed that momma spent much of her time praying for me. Thank God for a praying mother! Out of all the things, mom taught me, I can say without a shadow of a doubt that one of her substratum gifts to me was breathing and believing in our God. Mom did it in the way she responded to hardships and trials. She did it with graceful words, actions, prayers, and giving praise. I count this as the power to believe God can do anything. It is such an honor to have an advantage of Christian ethics.

A parent's daily prayer should be to thank God that their children are delivered from sin and deadly diseases. I don't know everything my mother prayed for, but I'll tell you this: He was near death. This story is a perfect example of how we should look to our heavenly Father whenever we feel trapped. If we pray and put our trust in God, He will rescue us from the traps that Satan has laid for us. And we also have to trust God and not get into fear when there are things we don't understand. God will never do anything except what is best for us. God not only delivers us from the snare laid by the trapper (Satan) but according to the last part of verse 3, He also delivers us from the deadly pestilence.

Do you see what the Psalmist is doing? If you're going to be protected in life, you'll have to dwell on God's character, the Most-High God above all things, the Almighty God who is great in grace and will always provide for our needs. The Lord, our Eternal God. Elohim! Some secret "hidden riches" places include wisdom to guide your life and ministry properly and knowledge to bless and help others.

For us to have Jesus Christ as the center of our lives, there must be an overthrow of something like a nail fastened in a sure place. Beloved, whenever Jesus Christ comes into the heart, there is a battle, strife, a struggle, a down casting of the image of sin, and then a setting up of the cross in its place. All men, by nature, have some kind of righteousness.

No man is so vile, but he still wraps himself up in his rags and cajoles himself into believing that he has some degree of spiritual or moral excellence. Before Christ can come into the heart, all this natural excellence must be torn to shreds. Every stone of the wall upon which we have built aforetime must come down, and the foundations must be utterly destroyed; before we shall ever build a right and surety for eternity upon the cornerstone of Christ Jesus.

All our conceit about our past righteousness must be completely overthrown. So, the question I ask you today is this; are we selective with God's promises when it comes to trouble? Or are we convinced that the authority of the Word of God, the medicine of Scripture, is enough for all our needs? If you dwell in God, my friend, you will have protection from Satan's traps. You will have inoculation from sin's diseases and the 'supernatural secret service' at your elbow. You will have victory over every enemy and complete protection in whatever befalls you. That is what God does for us when we dwell underneath His wing.

Our only hope for the future lies in this; that those who trust Jesus are in Jesus Christ's hand and that He can keep that which they commit to Him. Those who trust in Jesus have the promise that the Holy Spirit shall dwell in them and walk in them, writing a law upon their hearts, making their hearts new, molding their natures into the nature of Christ, causing them to hate evil and to choose that which is good. You will never kill a single evil passion through your strivings apart from the precious blood of Christ because He is-The Only Safe Place.

CHAPTER 4

Seeds

Jesus said it best:
"Let the children come to Me.
Don't stop them!
For the Kingdom of God belongs to those
who are like these children, I tell you
the truth, anyone who doesn't receive the
Kingdom of God, like a child
will never enter it."

Girl "I got butterflies," my mom tells me. She said. "Robert was tall and handsome and considerate and kind." They were introduced by a friend of his named Gary. She had no idea he had inquired about her. Perhaps he was sure of what he was looking for in her. He told his friend that he was going to marry her. The first time he asked her on a date, she said no. He didn't get angry. He just used a different approach. He waited a few weeks to call her. When he did call, he asked, "Would you like to go with me tomorrow night?" "What took you so long?" She asked.

"I was giving you time," He said. Their first date was a Miles Davis concert. They were unable to restrain themselves. They fell in love. Six months later, they were married. I always thought it was the most romantic story I'd ever heard, but mom didn't like it. She didn't think it was romantic at all. "I had to say yes. He wouldn't take no for an answer," She said. Life is not worth living if we do not know love. Dad left the army after getting married because he wanted to make a life with his family, and you couldn't do that in the military. Of course, I was proud of my dad for being a serviceman. Dad, my hero, was alive and home. I never had the fear he would leave us. That alone was comforting. He was honest, hardworking, and had excellent credit. Ladies date and marry someone willing to go the extra mile. I believe that love helps us reach our true destiny. Only love can heal the wounds of the past.

In Jesus, God made His love for us vital and real so that we might see it with our own eyes through others. God's real love for us in Jesus Christ is Unselfish. Ungrudging. Forgiving. Gracious. Embracing. Enduring. Sustaining. From the beginning, God planned to develop a people that reflected His character. And what is His character? *Love!* The one who remains in love remains in God, and I believe that is what God gave my mom and dad.

When we live in a relationship with God and stop and remember how much God loves us, it is easy to love God with all our hearts, soul, mind, and strength. He blends our pieces through all of the good times and difficult times. Mom needed Robert, and he needed her. The sooner we learn these vital principles, the richer and better our lives will be. But we must give before we receive.

A Gift

Although she married a wonderful man who was good to her and her children, she had so many emotional vicissitudes from her past that we did not know she was carrying, but he loved her past the hurt. He wanted us to know that he was not trying to take the place of our biological father. Robert wanted us to get to know him for who he was in our mother's life. God could have left my mother alone to raise us, but he chose not to. He knew she needed Robert in so many ways.

In my heart, I believe mom was honest with God when she prayed for a good-hearted and godly man, and God heard her prayers. When we understand that God can repair the hurting places in our lives, we will be more open to being honest before Him and others. In my opinion, Robert made our lives easy. He came into our lives at the right time. God knew who Robert was when He chose him to do what our biological father didn't do. Now, it takes a real man to come into a woman's life and help raise another man's children as his own. Growing up with both parents in the home is a blessing. That is nothing to boast about, but it is a fact of life.

There are many women worldwide whose hearts may have been broken by the absence of a father, and, unfortunately, some families did not have both parents. Today, I believe more women have chosen to be mothers without choosing fathers, not by choice. While in the meantime, other women have become single parents by necessity.

Reflecting on my childhood, I could see how my mom made that decision wisely and that I had someone to love me even though he was not our biological father. I had not met my biological father at this age in my life. Robert had a wealth of knowledge and was distinctively different. He also had some resistance. He did not come to us perfectly. No real man can enter an unfamiliar place without wounds if he does not survive. He was a soldier. As for me, he was my hero, and no one could tell me anything negative about him. If he ever had a bad day, we never knew it. He was a family man and loved spending quality time with us. His work was endless and often thankless, but in the end, it showed how sound and well-adjusted he raised us.

Robert didn't let us get away with a lot. I quickly learned one of the main characteristics of a good father is that he is a good disciplinarian. A good father makes all the difference in a child's life. He often disapproved of our misdeeds, using tough love to prove a point. When we did something out of the norm, he put us on punishment. Of course, I never liked punishment. I could not think straight. In my mind, my brothers got away with a lot. He proved his point through the power of words. He allowed us to make mistakes. As young as we were, I am almost sure he was open-minded, understanding us to change in a heartbeat. Our mood swings, our temper, and our sudden taste in food and clothing. He showed us our value.

Some parents are afraid of making their children mad. I can remember the first time I called myself pouting. My brothers had labeled me a 'daddy's girl,' and dad called me his 'one-in-a-million.' Amid my tantrum, we went back and forth, and I said, "I don't like you right now," and crossed my arms. He said, "Fine! Go to your room until you feel like you can like me again." The frown I wore sure didn't last long. That is how he disciplined me. The means of discipline are actions and words.

Parents are supposed to discipline us through their words, actions, warnings, and a few consequences (if needed) to keep us on track. Early on, it helped establish the principles of order in our family and protected us from things we could not see. I do not think my brothers liked some of the disciplinary actions. These sound teachings should also include sound doctrine. (Hebrews 12:5) says not to make light of God's actions and not to lose heart at His words of rebuke.

Many of us long for being reared in a peaceful home, and faith should be the center of it. Our world is so unstable, but the home is where the heart is and should be a shelter in the time of a storm. It is where children learn to grow up and be good Christians and where we forge our lives with respect and true unconditional love based on good relationships. We, as children, have a way of seeing our parent's moods, attitudes, and actions. We also have a way of imitating our parents, either in a good way or bad. It seems to me that many fathers are making a concerted effort to be exceptional fathers today.

How often have you heard the elders say, "You know, we grew up poor, but we sure didn't know it?" Why? I'm glad you asked; because there was a father in the home who did not complain about providing the basic needs for his family. He did not have much, but he provided. I do not recall when the lights, water, or phone were off. We had food, clothes, and a comfortable place to live. I think all children need Godly fathers. We never went hungry. Love always protects, love trusts, always hopes, and always perseveres. Love never fails. When you love children like this, your home will always have security. I could not compare my dad to another man. I depended on him for many things, and I appreciated that. He would always say, "I love you," and that he was proud of us. So many people would tell us how much he bragged about us. That was very affirming to me. A Godly man has a tremendous opportunity to teach his children the Word of God. Dad would read one of his favorite bible stories to me every night before bed. He and I both loved the story of Gideon (Judges 6- 7). In the end, he would say, *"Hey, Sport,* when you feel discouraged, distracted, or even defeated, remember the Lord is with you, mighty warrior. I want you to remember that you are a leader, and everybody can't go where God is taking you. Always let Jesus lead you no matter how hard it gets.

When you are faithful to God, He will be faithful to you as He was with Gideon." Let God fight for you. He said. Sometimes, I wonder how many children realize if they don't have an earthly Father; they do have a heavenly Father who never sleeps. Our Father will never leave us nor forsake us. He wants us to have everything we need. He knows what is best for us. He has our best interest at heart. There is so much security in a father's arms, whether you are a child or an adult. If you do not have a father, will you allow Jesus to wrap you in his arms? He will keep you safe from all hurt, harm, and danger. The only way to be a real father is to surrender your heart to Christ. Think about the influence you can have as a father on your children. Honor your father and mother so that it may be well with you, and you will live long on the earth. (Ephesians 6) Are you a Godly father? Here's my point. The father of Godly children has cause for joy. Build a legacy. Have high expectations. Laugh, talk and cry with your children. Be the dad. Be the hero. Be a Gift.

The 'Special Child'

Dad was a dramatic storyteller. I did tell you how dad told bedtime stories. Well, some were about him. He'd pause and chuckle at some memories. He always started slow, with lots of pauses. "Go on! What happened next?" I'd ask, even if I'd already heard that story before. It was special when he talked about his time stationed at Fort Hood, TX. I loved to hear him reminisce about his old times. Mom giggled or rolled her eyes when he told his stories and glared at her. If someone interrupted his storytelling, he got mad, and we had to beg him to continue and promise that no one would interrupt again. He always fought harder, flew faster, and gambled smarter than everyone else in his stories.

Along the way, he rescued women, children, and even men who weren't as strong and clever. He taught us the secrets of his heroics; he showed us how to straddle a wild hog and break his neck and where to hit a man in the throat so you could kill him with one powerful jab. But he assured us that as long as he was around, we wouldn't have to defend ourselves because, by God, "anyone who so much as laid a finger on any of Robert Lee's children was going to get their butts kicked so hard that you could read his shoe size on their butt cheeks." At some point, I must have drifted off because the next thing I knew, I was talking to someone. I was disoriented by the unfamiliar surroundings and the light that was shining. In the light, it was a looming reality. It was not bright, but enough to see someone standing afar reaching out to me. As I began to see clearer, we laughed. The voice was heavy but not too loud. The laughter woke me as I saw him standing at my bedside. He smiled. He had a dark complexion, a nicely groomed mustache, and was tall. He was dressed in liberty overalls, a light blue work dress shirt, and dark steel-toed boots. (The overalls threw me off)

"It is okay. Don't be afraid! "You are Ann's child?" He said.

"Yes, my mom is Dave Anna," I said.

Now, I'm sitting in bed, looking at the beautiful light.

"Yes, I know. I just came to tell you that you are Ann's special child," He said.

"What does he mean by special?" I mumbled. I'm smart!

45

"What's your name?" I asked. "I am D.C." He said. My thoughts paused. I've heard that name. *My grandfather!*

I only heard my mom and aunt tell us stories of their father. Especially how they both set fire to a hay field smoking rabbit tobacco. Yes, we laughed! Unfortunately, he died before I was born; before now, I had never seen a picture of him.

It was barely three in the morning. I called out to my mom and dad, who had probably just positioned themselves in their bed. "A man is in my room!" Immediately, my dad responded. "Where did he go?" Mom sat with me until he came back.

"Daddy, he didn't go outside," I said.

"Where did he go?" He asked.

"He left," I said. Both were shocked! Mom asked, "Toni baby, tell us what you saw?" I gave them small details of what I'd seen and said, he told me his name was D.C.

"That's my father!" Mom shouted.

I remember that moment so clear. I was nine years old when I experienced my first vision. Imagine being able to see an image of the past. God had given me an extraordinary ability to "see things," but I did not understand at this age. When I would tell my parents about the visions I saw, they did not ignore me. Instead, they paid attention and encouraged me to see things differently. When I had dreams that seemed to be premonitions about the future, my mom would smile and share a few of her own. Interestingly as it was, when older people recognized it, they called this particular one-*gifted.*

The gift is not the gift of suspicion or judgment. Like the other gifts of the Spirit, this gift is always for edification and building up the Body of Christ. Sometimes God speaks to us through our dreams and visions as a method of communication with the given ability to understand the vision. However, not all revelation comes from God; not everything that appears spiritual is from the Holy Spirit. (You better be careful with your gift!) These are called visitation dreams. It's something you wake up from, convinced the person you saw was there with you at your side. The dead will communicate with you very clearly and offer some sort of reassurance that they are okay or everything around you is okay. You'll wake up from these dreams not upset or scared but filled with a sense of peace and unbelievable love. From religious teachings, I learned that as messengers of the divine, some spirits and angels are wise counselors.

They can assist us in our spiritual growth. Believing in the Holy Spirit comforted me as a child when I felt overwhelmed by loneliness and sorrow. The solace of knowing I could speak my heart to God during these times made me feel less alone. Knowing that the angels were there with me, I had no reason to fear. They were there with me, listening to my tears and my heartache. I could not see them, but I knew they were there. Sometimes, I hear them whispering to me to let me know all would be well with my soul, speaking to my heart in a divinely sweet secret language.

The presence of angels, of angelic spirits, reminds us that there is a realm of mystery that cannot be explained by human intellect or will. We all experience this mystery in our daily lives in some ways, however small, whether we see ourselves as "spiritual" or not. We find ourselves in the right place at the right time, ready and able to receive blessings without knowing how we got there. Sometimes, God shows us things (dreams, aspirations, goals). Often, we wonder what God is doing. "Did I see or hear from God?" Is God trying to break through to you? Is he waking you up to a specific dream, aspiration, or goal? In my case, only God could show me as a spiritually gifted 'Special Child.'

Seeds

Although I enjoyed my friends in the village, I also spent summers with my grandparents, Lucy and Herbert. They are my dad's mother and father. My grandparents got married when they were in their twenties. My grandfather moved from Charleston, South Carolina, in 1938. He served in the United States Army for two and a half years. He stood about 5'9, had a slim frame, and he was the tallest man I thought I had ever seen.

After leaving the Armed Forces, he got a job as a supervisor at the local lumber company to help support his family. He knew the meaning of hard work and sacrifice. They lived in a rural neighborhood. It was a close-knit community where people were hard-working, independent and replete with family and friends. My grandfather would wake us every Saturday morning with grits, sausage, bacon, eggs, pancakes, homemade biscuits, and coffee on the breakfast table. He was honest. He was a hard worker, a provider, and a family and community man. He served as a deacon at his church and was the second person who taught me the Word of God. He taught me to memorize scripture, not just to recite words, but to internalize their meaning. The most significant distinction between him was the way he explained the scriptures. He had an intense but fading kind of scratchy voice. He sang the church's old hymns, such as Amazing Grace, Precious Lord, and at the Cross. They sure sounded good! Usually, close to the last line, I would chime in. He would look at me and smile with such grace.

One of the many lessons I will never forget is: "Child, whenever you want to give something to somebody, give the best in you, never the second best." He'd say, "God is not always in a temple, mosque, or church. He is with people! Prayers in cottages are as acceptable to Him as prayers in palaces. When you serve them with whatever you have, you have served God." He often told me, "Treat others how you want them to treat you." His sense of humbleness was contagious. He was a complex person, yet he taught me many simple things that are important for a child to know. For example, he taught me how to ride a horse, blow soap bubbles and tie a kite knot that met the challenge of the March winds. In time, he taught me about complex things too. He taught me about hopes and dreams. He taught me the love of words. His stories taught me patience, honor, courage, and commitment.

If I am helping anyone today, it is because of the teachings of this simple soul. I did not learn them in any school or college. Later in life, I would downplay the impact these childhood experiences had on my development. It is incredible how God can put so much in so little. Even in the most painful situations and circumstances, we are marvelous in God's hands. Without his teachings, without his words, my words would not have been. Granddad used wisdom while planting word seeds, which has stayed with me ever since.

My grandparent's house was a special place to be. Being there had its perks because granddad was so easygoing. The house always seemed to have something that set it apart from all the rest. As you walk into the house's front door, you notice a long, slender hallway that leads into the dining room. The pungent smell of tobacco was quite evident when you reached this point. Yes, my grandfather did

48

smoke, and he chewed tobacco. The house was always full of laughter. Our family called it the Ashley fillin' station. There was always someone visiting, whether it was family or friends. My grandfather's door was always open to everyone, no matter what. In the summer, whoever happened to be at the house would sit on the back deck with my grandfather. They would talk for hours about anything and everything imaginable. He was known as the neighborhood watchman. He always had an ear-to-ear smile that would brighten up anyone's day if it was not going too well. He was always willing to lend a hand in anything that someone needed. He was a highly giving person to everyone around him and never asked for anything in return. He was spontaneous; he did what he wanted to at the drop of a hat, and nobody ever stopped him and would not let a job go until he was delighted with it.

From time to time, he played sports. A little softball kept him in shape, the more physical, the better. He was always active in gardening, farming, and cooking, but he always had time for the ones he loved. He was a farmer. He had an abundance of pigs, cows, a few goats, and two horses named Jack and Red. We also had Chip, a west highland terrier dog. Small in height and weighed about twenty pounds, if that. Despite his size, he was watchful of our surroundings and me. Friendly, robust, and spirited may even chase a cat or two when he feels like it.

On the other hand, my grandmother had her fair share of stories but never told any. Her stories were about the way she would eat. She savored her food and cherished it. She was seldom outwardly affectionate. She didn't need to be. At just five feet tall, she was the kind of woman you saw on the street and knew to move out of her way. Her demeanor was strict; her hands were tied with thick blue veins crisscrossing over her thin, frail fingers. I remember holding her hands as a child, how delicate and soft they seemed, yet that never made them seem any less worn or sturdy. Her hands told stories of different times, of different worlds and hardships. She had grown up worlds away from me, in a different land, at a different time, in an era and life that I would never know. When I wrapped my arms around her petite frame, afraid I would break her, she responded with strength disproportionate to her size.

Although she held tightly, like she was holding on for dear life, and then she would let go, she smiled and moved on. She also had this look in her eyes that I could not figure out. My grandmother had little education, but she could run several businesses. Before moving to Alabama, she managed independently with my grandad and my dad. Her stories were in her complaints. Grandma constantly complained of severe stomach pain. She knew something was wrong, but every time she went to the doctor, the doctor would blame the pain on acid reflux or indigestion. All I knew was that something was terrible, causing her a lot of pain. Because of the constant pain she was in, she was almost always on painkillers, which caused her to sometimes make her forget who we were. I have one vivid memory of when I walked into her room, but she didn't know who I was and screamed at me to get out.

For a nine-year-old, I didn't understand what was happening. It hurt me when grandma did this. She often got mad at minor things. My grandad kept telling me that she didn't mean it and wasn't herself at that moment, but I still couldn't understand. I tried to keep a smile so my grandmother would not notice. I was just a kid who knew something was very wrong. Most of my time was spent reading or sitting on the porch with Chip. Now and then, amusement came for him to bark and chase at a car in passing, no further than the mailbox. After his chase, he'd look at me as if to say, "Now you do something!" Throw a stick. Throw a ball. Run. Do something. So, I threw the ball, and we did that for a while until I heard the phone ring during our happy time.

In those days, we did not have caller id. So if you missed a call, you just missed it. She could not get to it as fast as I could. I answered. "Hello, Ashley residence." *"Hey, sport!"* Daddy! "What are you up to?" "Are you being a good girl?" He asked. Grandma could not wash her hands fast enough. I was holding back the tears when I said, "Yes." "Sounds good!" He said. "Are you on your way to pick me up?" I asked. "I'll be there tomorrow after work, and will you give the phone to grandma?" He asked. I yelled in excitement. "Grandma, my daddy wants to speak with you!" Tomorrow could not come fast enough. The weeks were getting longer. I was on cloud ten.

While grandma was talking, I needed something to amuse Chip and me, so we snooped and found the hydrant. *Don't laugh!* I know you drank from the house hose pipe on a hot summer day. That was the best water, and I was thirsty! After I had my share, I gave some to Chip. It was nice and cold. The livestock filtration system was separate from the house. Grandad had to keep the cattle and horses hydrated with fresh, clean water. The cattle alone could consume 15-30 gallons, depending on their body weight. Watering livestock during the summer months was a job.

I heard, "Turn that water off, girl! And "Why are your clothes so dirty?" I looked down and didn't realize they were dirty. She made me nervous, and I'd stammer. "I'm s-s-s-sorry," I said. Chip ran off and left me. *Lil'- Punk*, I could not believe what I was hearing. I had never seen my grandmother angry. She was furious! She said, "Your mom didn't pack enough clothes for you." Do you know what I did? Yes! I rolled my eyes, but she saw it and spanked me.

Chip whimpered with sorrow from the screen door. She quickly dismissed me when the phone ranged. It was one of her lady friends, but my face lit up when I saw granddad walk in the door. Hey, "Granny! What's the matter?" He asked. Before I could get the words, I wanted to go home. He asked, "Is that your daddy on the phone?" "No, sir," I said. Well, "Let's see when we can get you home. I'll call your dad when she gets off her call." He said. He always solved my problems. When I returned home that summer, Mom asked, "Did you enjoy your stay?" It was not a conversation piece. But I shared how much I enjoyed church and was ready to be baptized.

Why This Bitter Cup?

By my next visit, my grandfather had retired after twenty-five years. He still had a good memory, but grandma repeated the same questions. It was evident that they weren't as energetic. Aging is not a condemnation but a blessing! He had hogs, but the garden was lifeless. I saw him sitting alone with an expression of unutterable sorrow or exhaustion. I asked, "What are you thinking about?" "Oh, nothing," He said. I hugged and squeezed him tight with a small pat on the back. He smiled. A month later, my dad found granddad sitting on the floor in his bedroom. We did not know how long he had been there. Grandma had no idea.

He told my dad he missed his medications and was feeling dizzy. Due to that unexpected incident, granddad was taken to the hospital in the middle of the night by ambulance. This time was different and seemed to averbate his heart issues. He had recently been diagnosed with CHF (Congestive Heart Failure). After a series of tests, he had pneumonia, even worse, tuberculosis. The congestion that occurred in his lungs made it difficult for him to breathe. By the end of that week, he began to get weaker. I knew then he was slipping away.

Meanwhile, grandma moved in with us, which was emotional, especially for my mom. Mom divided her time trying to meet my dad's needs, her children, and now her new housemate. As she adjusted, mom had to help grandma maintain normalcy and independence. Mom never wavered. This arrangement only served to turn mom into an even stronger woman of faith who never left our side. Through this living arrangement, I quickly learned from a young age that the world did not revolve around me.

Temper tantrums were instantly shut down because I should have behaved better for grandma. Despite all this, I was taught what love was about our family sacrifices and putting others before you. Mom had become grandma's sole advocate, caretaker, and everything. She made sure she treated her as if she was not a burden until grandma had spoken ill of her to my dad behind her back, which of course, mom did not appreciate.

Before she moved in, they never did have long-winded conversations, but now that she was with us, she insisted on helping mom with whatever she needed, but clearly, she was saddened by granddad's state now. In her sadness, she did not stop radiating to mom with her attitude, and it seemed like her drive to help was fueled by the fact that she had someone to vent to while doing so.

The next few days, mom took offense when grandma-starting asking, "is the food ready yet? I am hungry." Mom replied with a cut tone, "I am working on it. I cannot cook any faster." Grandma said, "Oh, you don't want to cook for me? I see." All of this happened when dad was not there to hear it, and when he was, grandma never said anything to mom. One day I heard mom crying and talking in a meek and quiet tone. What could I do to stop grandma from constantly venting and taking her frustrations out on mom?

It got to the point where mom asked me to start recording their conversations to let dad know what is going on because she did not want to talk back to grandma because of her unconditional respect for the elderly. Yes, I know we all should generally understand our elders, but to me, it looked like grandma tried to place a guilt trip on mom with petty stuff that was causing her a lot of stress and anger. As you can imagine, when mom and dad brought up the possibility of grandma moving to an assisted living, she said she would be fine going back home just like she was before she had to stay here. Besides, she said, "I don't want to go live with no old people anyway."

At the time, grandma was sixty-nine years old. After many discussions, dad and mom said, "Ok, they let her go back to her house and hired someone as her caregiver until granddad got better. This situation was very hard on my parents. My parents supported grandma as best as they could. They both worked full-time and could only do so much. My dad was the only child, so there was no other support besides mom and us, the children. A few weeks after grandma returned home, she called dad every day.

Not my will, but Your Will

This particular day started like any other day, but by the end of it, I knew my life would never be the same. Grandad became worse late in the night. The nurse called that morning for the family to come to the hospital. The hospital was about five miles away. We could make it there in time. I saw the emergency response equipment and lights flashing as we entered through the double door. Then I heard the dreadful, Code blue! Complete silence fell.

My ears popped when I heard the doctor say, "I am sorry, Mr. Ashley, we did everything we could." Granddad took his last breath at exactly 11:30 am on Thursday, March 23, 1989. He was seventy-four. I mourned his loss but hated the month of March. One of the tragedies of childhood is that it's only in retrospect that we get a sense of how complex the adults in our lives truly were. I will never forget watching the tears flow from my dad's eyes. Our family was devastated. I woke up that morning still having a granddad and left not having one. A piece of my heart was *irrevocably* broken. Up until his passing, I had never had to deal with the death of someone so close to me.

Sure, I'd been to a few funerals by then, but I never understood what was happening. My granddad's death opened my eyes to what death meant. I wasn't going to be able to see one of my favorite people anymore. I would never be able to drink the last sip of his coffee again when it gets cold.

Following his death, grandma started going through his collections of old videotapes and radios, pulling out photo albums and passing them around to everyone in the living room. But there was one she handed just to me, a thin blue album with a floral cover I didn't recognize. She said she wanted me to have it as if she expected me to recognize it. But I'd never seen it before. I flipped it open and found a sheet of notebook paper. In marker, in grandad's handwriting, was, *The Fun I Had this Summer with my granddaughter Toni* - H.L. Ashley. I missed seeing my grandad all the time, and his death showed me what it was like to have someone you care about to be ripped away from you. His death showed me a horrible pain that I didn't even know would be possible then. It felt like I had lost the one person who held us together.

Over the years, I miss him something terrible, but time has somewhat lessened the grief. In addition to our relationship with God, we should also cultivate our relationships with others: first of all, by showing affectionate concern for our families, our children, and grandchildren, but also for the poor and those who suffer, by drawing near to them with practical assistance and our prayers. We have grown in humanity by caring for others, and now we can be teachers of a way of life that is peaceful and attentive to those in greatest need. Like seeds, blessings multiply; even though the seed leaves our hand, it never leaves our life.

Seeds

By: Elizabeth Morgan

The Bible says: that God created the

heavens and the earth

first and yet, at the same time,

he brought Herbert from the dust.

Your mind and body are complete

, but your spirit is under God's control.

You found your purpose in this life,

Winning souls to Jesus Christ.

Lord, I appreciate the adoration Herbert Lee Ashley

bestowed. You're in the arms of Jesus now

for the love, joy, and peace you showed.

Your mind was a garden that helped plant *'seeds.'*

Now, I understand what sowing and reaping mean.

CHAPTER 5

Scars that Heal

Thou shalt not be afraid for the terror by night;
nor for the arrow that flieth by day;
Nor for the pestilence that walketh
in darkness; nor for the destruction
that wasteth at noonday
(Psalm 91: [5-6])

Fear is a powerful, controlling, paralyzing emotion.
This verse does not claim that you will not encounter terror,
arrows, pestilence, and destruction, but it says you need not
fear these things

$\mathcal{W}e$ love a good scar story. A story of an old wound now healed up. Stories of people who have overcome adversity. Stories of people's growth after facing a life challenge. They don't want people with open wounds. Those who are still struggling on the way with wounds not yet thoroughly scarred over. What about you and your scars? What stories do they tell? What pain do they still hold? Some heal. Some don't. Scars are a consequence of an injury. Scars also arise from offenses. These offenses come through people who mistreat us and injure our hearts. But for me, I was damaged. And I never talked about any of it. Throughout grade school, I endured different types of bullying. Some of it was subtle. Some of it is overt. All of it is humiliating.

I have a good scar story I would like to share: On the left side of my lip, I carry a jagged scar from the first day of third grade. After the bell ranged, seconds later, I heard the jeers, "Cripple! You're a cripple. You don't belong here!" Two boys started throwing rocks, and I felt the sting of gravel hitting my back. It scattered along the path. I looked up to see who they were, but they were hidden.

One of them started kicking me and laughing. Blood was running down my forehead and flowing out of my nose. My knees and elbows were scraped raw and covered with sand. I was still holding the Snicker bar, but I had smashed it during the fall, tearing the wrapper and squeezing out the creamy caramel filling, which was also covered with grit. The short, heavy-set boy stepped out of the shadows as the pelting continued. He laughed as he imitated my pronounced limp. I have genu valgum (knocked knees), a large gap between my feet when I stand with my knees together. I tried to maintain my balance but collapsed on the pavement within seconds. Immediately the boys dispersed, and it was silent.

The area was deserted. I was alone. My whole body felt sore. Just nine years old. Seethed with fury, I wanted to retaliate. I began taking karate lessons with some vague idea that I would become strong enough to get my revenge. Holding grudges and fantasizing about getting even made me feel weaker, not stronger. Since I encountered cruelty so frequently, I almost came to expect it. No one ever stood up for me. Even when I was bullied in front of others, they looked the other way.

They didn't want to get involved, and I didn't expect anything different. Because I never told anyone about being harassed, I concluded what was happening. And over time, the power of those conclusions became magnified and deeply ingrained. I told myself that something was wrong with me. I was the outcast. That's what a scar is! I think this is important because most of us carry our scars hidden deep within, out of sight of others and even ourselves. It's the natural process of wound healing. In fact, in most instances, we are told at some point that when sharing personal stories, it's good to talk about your scars but not your open wounds. It can make us all uncomfortable to come face-to-face with someone's open wound. But we love a good scar story.

The stories of the mountain scaled, addictions overcome, anger transformed, and the hole we felt filled with something new. And we prefer these stories shared in retrospect after the painful worst is over. But rarely is life this clean and separated between past and present wounds. And rarely are our deepest wounds ever fully healed and scared over.

We all know the little rhyme: Sticks and stones will break my bones, but names will never hurt me. That statement expresses how we can be in the midst of trouble yet not let that same trouble touch or harm us. It is the ability to sing during the waves and the billows: 'It is well with my soul.' We all know a simple statement so well, yet behind it is a profound philosophy. You know that the sticks and the stones may touch you, they may cut your flesh, they may do all sorts of pain and bruises to your body, but you know that if people call you names that there's a choice of whether to listen to them or not, whether to let them affect you or penetrate your heart and hurt you.

The way you and I handle being rejected and wounded is critical. Some have left the church because they believe that the church pretends to be something it isn't, dressing up its scars and covering up its wounds, and not dealing with real issues and challenges of life. They believe they won't be welcomed with their scars and their own scar stories. Our response can lead to healing to even more hurt. Almost everyone I know has been wounded to one degree or another. It doesn't matter if a person is young or old, rich or poor, intelligent or ignorant, healthy or infirm, educated or illiterate.

Who Made the Difference?

The third and fourth grades were challenging for me, but I noticed something beautiful happening on the inside. Subtle changes and I understood more about the power of the written Word. I had the desire to start *writing*. Journaling became an intimate place that stripped me of myself. A secret ambition took root. I needed to place on paper what existed in my heart. It allowed me to look back at what I learned in school and what I wanted to pursue in the following days, months, and years. Journaling helped me be honest with myself and conscious of my actions and habits. I enjoyed being quiet - my family didn't bother or probe me. Quiet. It was a nice place to be.

Eventually, journaling led me to identify the blind spots I wanted to improve. I asked myself questions every day. Some were easier than others, while others were uncomfortable. For example, is there something I could do better today? If so, what? I wrote about things that I struggled with. Reading was one because I hated talking. I was afraid of saying things that would not come out right. I had a stutter with a lisp falling short of 'S' words. If I didn't get a good night's sleep, I felt it would be one of those "bad" days with my speech. P-p-p-*please*...

Schoolwork was never a problem. Classes were easy, and learning was fun. Mrs. Bonifay was a tiny ball of energy with a high-pitched voice. There was no doubt as to her power and authority in that classroom. She made every day an adventure, and I hated to miss school, even when I was sick.

During the reading sessions, I felt isolated. The jokes were more hurtful, and problems were solved by telling the teacher. It took me some time to get used to the more peaceful approach, but I liked it once I did. One day I slid quietly into the room, only a couple of minutes late, and grinned at Mrs. Bonifay, noticing my tardiness but said nothing. "Today," she began, "we're going to continue talking about the writer named Shakespeare. How long ago did he live?" she asked the class.

"Four hundred years ago!" they responded immediately. "How many plays did Shakespeare write?" Thirty-seven! I had no idea that Shakespeare was not usually taught in third grade. Mrs. Bonifay simply offered it, and the rest of my class and I absorbed it.

Every Tuesday, she told us about Shakespeare's time-about kings and castles, as well as about the rats and fleas that lived in the straw most people used for bedding. I listened fascinated and entranced by her stories, which taught me history, literature, math, and science without me even being aware. She passed out a children's version of Hamlet, full of pictures and explanations, and let me read the play and act out the fight scenes. I always had a passion to learn. Also, being the curious one I always asked questions. Asking questions was not to embarrass me. But my refusal to ask could lead to unnecessary aggravation.

One of the lessons Jesus taught us is to: Ask, and it shall be given you; seek, and ye shall find; knock, and it shall be opened unto you. (Matthew 7:7) This scripture reminds me of how Peter stood out from the crowd of disciples. Always asking questions he did not understand. Even as the disciples sat with Jesus, they listened, observed and learned through the parables from Him. I believe Jesus' teaching has had such an effect on them that it showed every aspect of how He "the teacher" lived. When God does certain things in our lives that may appear random, we think less of ourselves and take a different direction. Remember, you will never get answers, if you don't observe and ask questions.

Every day went quickly in Mrs. Bonifay's class and she often stayed after school with a few of us to make cookies or build projects. As my learning increased, I established a student/teacher relationship with all my teachers. I had a secret code with my teachers. A "thumbs up" in the morning meant I was having a great day. A "thumbs down" meant "Please don't call on me. Short answers are better today." Soon, words flew off my tongue more easily when I had to read aloud in reading groups.

Just when I thought I was making good progress momma had a parent/teacher conference. Of course, back then, you had to visit the book fair while your teacher spoke with your parents about report cards. I wanted to know what they would talk about, so I stood outside the door and listened. Mrs. Bonifay asked, "Does Elizabeth talk much at home? We can hardly get her to sound words in the classroom. I know she is a smart girl. She knows how to write well." Took me by surprise!

My mom said, "She stammers when she speaks at home, and we have a speech therapist, Mrs. Weatherly, who comes to the house once a week." AWW, man! My secret was out. I did not want my teacher or classmates to know I was a stutterer. Mrs. Bonifay thought that may have been the case for my fear of speaking in class. "That's wonderful that you have already started speech therapy with her. I give her time to talk and respond in the classroom. I can tell when she is having trouble getting her words out. On those days, I try not to call on her and check on her written assignments instead.

If you could sign this paper, I could have Mrs. Weatherly continue her therapy here at the school. Momma signed the forms as Mrs. Bonifay went over my grades. "I expect a lot from your daughter. The same as I would from any student," she said. For the rest of the day, I wondered, "what was a pathologist, and why did I have to have one?" That next day, I didn't want to go to school. I felt like hiding under my bed all day. In the middle of class, Mrs. Weatherly, the speech pathologist, came to Mrs. Bonifay's classroom door and asked for me. We were getting ready to make our last castle out of popsicle sticks. Mrs. Bonifay stooped down and looked into my eyes. She whispered, "I'll ensure you have enough time to make your castle later."

Mrs. Weatherly and I met every Tuesday afternoon for therapy. I never missed a reading session, thanks to Mrs. Bonifay. My classmates did not know where I went when I left the room. They didn't need to know. Besides, Mrs. Weatherly was nice. She helped me relax, face a mirror, and breathe. She had me speak into a tape recorder to find out what letters were hard to say. I learned to speak slowly. '*Ssss*' was no problem after a while. I was beginning to feel good about myself, but I sure was going to miss Mrs. Bonifay and Mrs. Weatherly the following year.

One day during lunch, I didn't know Mrs. Weatherly was standing behind me in the cafeteria line. They were serving cheeseburgers, and I wanted one. When the lunch lady asked me, "What would you like, honey?" I clutched my tray and breathed heavily, "A-h-h-h-h, s-s-s-s" I could not get it out. The girl next in line (who my peers later gave the nickname Cheese) put her hand on my lips and demanded, "Will you get it out? I'm hungry!" I pursed my lips and exclaimed, "Burger, please!" I felt myself get hot inside from being embarrassed. Tears welled up in my eyes. I wanted to disappear. People can be so cruel and brutal, can't they?

Mrs. Weatherly took me to the lunch lady to explain what had happened, and she gave me an extra cheeseburger. Mrs. Weatherly even sat at the table with me to eat her lunch. Her calm, soft voice put me at ease. I shared with her how much I was missing my niece. Now, I stuttered more than I expected. It seemed to be getting the best of me. Then she said, "You know, Elizabeth, many famous people had problems speaking as you do. I think we both know you love to read. Your teachers tell me you write like you are painting a picture. Did you know that legendary actor James Earl Jones also had difficulty speaking? He never let it stand in his way, and neither should you. Do you know what else I think? Keep it up.

The day will come when you will be the author of books to inspire many people. I saw Mrs. Weatherly ten years ago at a book signing. A slender older lady came up to me. Her silver hair was in a bun like she always wore at school. She knew who I was. I knew who she was as soon as I saw her. I hugged her close to me, kissed her soft cheek, and whispered thank you. Mrs. Weatherly! You were the one: Who Made the Difference.

Scars Do Heal

These are just a few of my earliest experiences of feeling hurt and alienated by God's people. They may seem mild all these years later, but I remember them keenly because of how much they hurt at the time because they were the first of many such experiences to come. For years, I'd constantly check my mental Rolodex and pull this card when life mirrored the expression, *"You'll never amount to anything."* My high school, History teacher said to me, staring over her need-a-new pair of wire glasses. "AND such a pretty girl," she concluded as she turned and walked away. Her church skirt caught the wind and brushed my leg as she spun in a move that would make the Wicked Witch of the West proud. I stood in the hall, silent, frozen, allowing her words to seep into my pores.

They were such harsh words for a teenage girl who chased love through the halls of a school where love didn't live. My infraction: I'd lied about having permission to see the film "The Breakfast Club" because my high school crush was going.

A crush that never noticed me because my look didn't match that era's admired golden tones, a much harsher truth than this teacher bestowed. It's sobering to contemplate the impact that a stern, unattractive, unloving, unkind adult can have on a child, especially when that person is considered a mature Christian. And I learned the hard way that wounds inflicted on us, even if they are only wounds resulting from the laceration of words, can make us physically ill, but scars do heal! Scars and wounds are the means through which we enter other people's hearts. They are meant to teach us to become compassionate and wise.

When we refuse to let go of the pain in our systems, we become depressed. The toxic energy of depression fuels our opposing attitudes toward others and further drain our resources. Soon we project onto others the causes of our failure and blame them for our pitiable condition. This irresponsible response to our problems becomes ordinary and routine. I started to notice scars more as I looked around. I learned it is often good to ask people about their scars as long as I ask respectfully and lovingly. Asking demystifies scars and allows people to share what has shaped them because all scars have a story. When we display our scars, we inspire others to do the same. Something is captivating about people who are unafraid to be themselves: authentic, unmasked, and unashamed of the wounds that shaped them. Their vulnerability is magnetic.

Nevertheless, those with scars should wear them like jewels, treasured reminders of what we've endured. It's okay to show our imperfections. It is even courageous. And perhaps we'll discover the beauty in our scars. They show others what we've endured. God showed me through scripture that just as the man born blind, He would use my handicap for His glory. This revelation profoundly changed me as I saw my life through a new lens. One that was bigger than my comfort. Maybe not physically imprinted, but impactful. And what about the literal internal scars, losses, and griefs, or changes to lives that are lived into a new normal left from this coronavirus as we cannot return to the way things used to be? Maybe that's one of the reasons the bible has so much to say about wounds. And the wounded!

I believe that within the Word of God, one of the greatest ways that God has of revealing Himself to a dying world is through the witness of believers when they have trouble in life. Throughout scripture, we feel the pain, we hear the cries and we see the revenge. Often we observe the wounded becoming wounders' with the repeated cycle from person to person and generation to generation. But throughout the gripping narratives, God's love is contrasted with the pain like sunlight emerging in silver streaks from behind a blackened cloud. Because God's love not only comforts and redeems, it heals.

The question posed by the Spirit of God and the Psalmist here in 91:5-6 is this. How do you behave when trouble hits your life? A troubled life that is perplexing, stressful, and anxious with all the threats that are on our bodies and soul. When we come into suffering: how do we cope? Do you cope? Do you go to pieces, or do you go to God? Is there a way God has given us so we might survive without a scratch?

It has always been remarkable to me that the disciples recognized Jesus when they saw His scars. And you know Thomas needed to feel the Lord's nail wounds to verify that the risen Savior was before him. Jesus didn't need to have scars on His resurrected body. It is not just a passing detail that the one we call Lord and Savior, Jesus Christ, is resurrected with the scars of His traumatic and violent end still imprinted upon His body. His body could have been perfect, unblemished, and unscarred, but He chose to keep His scars so His disciples could validate His identity.

More importantly, they could be assured that He had conquered death. God chose not to erase these marks of death, the wounds of His love for us, so our Savior will always be known by His scars. Rather than physical imperfections, Jesus's scars are breathtakingly beautiful. They represent His love and our salvation. As I considered these truths, something stirred in me. Our scars are significant and precious. We shouldn't keep hiding them. They recognize us. They make us unique.

They are an integral part of who we are. They show that through Christ, we are conquerors that we have suffered and, by the power of the Holy Spirit, have overcome. Our scars remind us that God is sufficient and that physical perfection is not our goal. A life lived to God's glory is infinitely more valuable. Christ's scars become part of our story, and our scars become a part of God's story in our lives.

The scars of Christ become scars of hope as we deal with our wounds in life. There are some scars we love to show off and others we want to be sewn up as neatly as possible so that no one ever knows. Yet scars, whether visible or not, are something we all have in common, something everyone shares. We all have experienced pain both physically and emotionally in our lives. Yet, we are so often reluctant to share them. We, the people of God, are called to be the Body of Christ, broken and healed by God's grace and love.

We are a scarred and broken people with a scarred and broken Savior who has died and been raised for us all. In Christ, our wounds are healed, our sins are forgiven, and we are given a second chance at a new life-even new life with old scars. Without them, we would be less than real, less than "authentic." Without them, Jesus would be less than the one who had suffered, died, and conquered death for us. With them, Jesus stands with us as one who has been scarred by suffering and death yet is alive among us. Who better to lift the burden of our scars than this Jesus, our life, our hope, and our Lord?

At this point, Thomas says to Jesus, "Let me see your scars. That is how I know you are real." "Here, take a look! See!" (John 20:24-27). But there Jesus is, showing us His nail-scarred hands. "Take a look. See, it is me!" He had seen it with his own eyes. It was as real as the ground he walked on. No sense wasting time hoping that it had been a dream. It was too good to be true. I mean, really. A man rose from the dead? Our scars remind us of who we are. They tell a story of seasons or years, or journeys. For some, the scars prompt us to be thankful. "God was with me. No reason you should've survived that crash." For others, the scars are a constant reminder of pain. The hip replacement you had wasn't successful. Cancer took part of your ear and throat. Those scars tell a story of humanity's sin and God's suffering. It was also why Thomas had to see them.

He needed to encounter Jesus and see the wounds, the healed ones. So Jesus showed up. "Put your finger here and see my hand. It's me, Thomas." Jesus offered His body as proof. And at that moment, Thomas had what he needed. Do you have what you need? He is real! He has Risen! He has Risen! Indeed. What scars are we hiding that Jesus already knows about and sees? The fact that Jesus still has His nail scars reminds us of unrestrained love. And His scars didn't keep Him down. Because of this, whether our scars are physical or emotional don't have to keep us down. The wounds and scars in your life, on your body, in your heart, on your psyche, and those to come are scars that will remain as a point of strength. They are there as a reminder of your truth, an emblem of God's love for you who will see you through.

Our wounds disappear in the new life Jesus offers. They shrink when we allow others to help us navigate our scars. Life is full of hardships and heaviness. All of us have experienced trial and pain. All of us are living life wounded and scarred. We learn to deal with our wounds and press forward, but whether we acknowledge it or not, wounds and scars change us. We have the promises of God to help us in difficult days and the Holy Spirit within us.

One thing that fascinates me about Jesus' ministry; is the passion for God many people gained after He healed them. Our emotional, spiritual, physical, or internal wounds are all opportunities to welcome God. They are opportunities to welcome Jesus into our pain because the wounds we carry are where the light enters. The wounds we carry are the door that Jesus desperately wants to enter. Those wounds Jesus Himself felt, He continues to feel year after year, day after day, and He empathizes with us in our pain.

You know how we always hear in church that Jesus feels with us, He suffers with us? And sometimes, we can hear that so much that it may lose its value. Healing is an ongoing process. It isn't the same as curing. Healing is what happens to us, pulls us, and leads us to lean toward others and God, which pulls us to even greater healing. By His grace, we are not meant to stay wounded.

We are supposed to move through our tragedies and challenges. We are here to help each other through painful episodes of our lives. We can't remain stuck in the power of our wounds. We block our transformation. We overlook the greater gifts inherent in our wounds, the strength to overcome them, and the lessons we are meant to receive through them. We cling to the negative events and relationships from our past and present because they allow us to see ourselves as victims and everyone else as the source of our misery. Why is it so hard to give up a wound? We are all born with a certain packet of perceptions of "that which we know to be true." And the reality is that we are more afraid of change.

66

Change is hard, but God doesn't change. People do. When people change, God creates a new way to work with them. What He has never stopped doing is creating. He never changes. We do not have to only be people who minister from well-healed scars, but people who can minister even out of our wounded-ness, uncertainty, and fear. Sometimes sharing our wounds is the most authentic and helpful way to minister.

Maybe our journeys meander because going in a straight line might be dangerous; too much energy and change for us to process and embrace. We might wipe out too much in trying to get somewhere fast. We want it to be over. We want to rush to the end. Through our mistakes and our fears, we are called to be imperfect instruments of God's perfect love. Jesus' scars take over our scars and bring us new life. He is a wounded healer bringing peace. Jesus is our Lord, and our God, in the glory of the resurrection, still bears the wounds of His experience of God with us on earth. The resurrection did not remove His human experience.

There was something about wounds. Those scars were revelatory about who this was; not a ghost, not an apparition, not a trick that someone else had been executed in His stead, but that it was Him and was a Him with a capital "H" Jesus their Lord and so much more than just Him, but God. It wasn't His restored and fully healed body, but His scarred body, the evidence of His ordeal, that was somehow the revelatory sign of who He was. The scars told the story and revealed the truth. Without them, Jesus was a great teacher, a storyteller, and a wise conveyor of truth. With them, he was the embodiment of a love so profound that it died for us. As it was in the beginning, so it is today. The risen Lord still bears on His body the scars that speak of His solidarity with human suffering in all forms. These scars remind us that God is with us through all things, especially the appalling, destructive, and death-dealing times.

We don't have a God who stands at a distance, but rather one who entered fully into the reality of our pain. So when we suffer, we know that Christ can say, "I've been there, and I have the wounds to prove it." That's why our faith enables us to go on, in the name of Christ, despite our wounds. Just know that Jesus experienced all these things in his own life. We don't have to pretend that we are all right. Each of us has a unique personality, and the dimensions of our personality speak to our limits. You see, Jesus' scarred hands are reaching out to show us God not only understands our suffering but has taken our suffering into His very own body. We must always remember that Jesus' hands are evidence of Scars That Heal. God brings new life to our scars. In our vulnerability, we must continue to meander together so that healing and hope might flow through us and into the world.

CHAPTER 6
What Now?

"I will reach out my hand,
trusting that life reaches toward me,
bringing me comfort and strength to prevail.
When the time comes, I will be ready."
~' Lil Brat.'

Someone once said, "The only time a goodbye is painful is when you know you will never say hello again," and little did I know how painful it would be. Look, I get it. Change is hard. But I'm here to tell you it's not impossible. In time, we will be helpers for others. We believe good living results in good things happening for us. This thought is a comforting idea when things are going well. If we are in good health, our family is doing well, and work or retirement is enjoyable, we want to believe in this. It gives us a part to play in our blessings. We have been good and faithful, so we are reaping the rewards. When we make good choices, we insulate ourselves from some problems. Then, just like in Job's case, we think, "What did I do wrong?"

That's certainly a part of my story.

It seemed my sister was flying off to New Jersey yesterday, determined to make a better life for her family. I haven't seen my sister in twelve years, but we finally built a bond during those years. I missed her so much. It was a small step but a step in the right direction. I talked with her several times since the move, and we were both emotional each time. Pausing on several occasions as we talked about the goodness of God and how faithful He is. The bond of our sisters shared faith. It touched my heart to the core. In our conversations, I could tell she was unhappy. When I say unhappy, I mean *unhappy*.

At age fifty, her heart had already been broken. It was in no condition to give to another man. There was no shortage of men over the years-men looking to rescue her, sweep her off her feet, and give her the life they felt she longed for. But after a relationship betrayal, my sister had no desire to marry. At the time, she worked several jobs to make ends meet. She had always been fairly straightforward, naturally sophisticated, and quiet. But without question, her world revolved around taking care of her home and my niece. I couldn't have imagined it then, but that phone call was marked for her return home. Only God understood her pain, and even then, He was reaching His Holy hands around her, comforting her with a peace that passed all understanding (Philippians 4:6). I think it was God's peace that had finally convinced her to call home.

It was the only reason she had survived. How had it begun? Like everything with mothers and daughters. When mom answered the phone, my sister had almost been too choked up to speak. Why did I have to be the one to hear their conversation? I heard my sister say: "I, I should have called sooner, but, well." She uttered a soft, exasperated huff, "I should have called." But mom was nothing but gracious. Then, I heard, "Thank you." The tears came down, streams of them. I didn't mind, and I didn't try to stop them this time.

When you want something, you will find a way. When you don't want something, you'll find an excuse. Talking about the possibility of a child returning home can be emotional. Mom retrieved a cup from the cabinet to pour herself a cup of coffee. After a sip of her coffee, she couldn't help but tell me they were returning. "What do you feel?" I asked. I felt her smile start in her heart and fill her face. She looked at me and said, "Toni baby, you're a gift. You always have been." I chuckled. Before she could say anything else, dad's voice from the hall interrupted us. "Hey!" "Are the biscuits ready?" We both grinned and set a place for him to sit at the table.

A comfortable silence settled between them for a long moment. Mom settled back in her chair and said, "Robert, when I knew the situation, I didn't hesitate. I was going to tell you today that the children will be here in June." Dad smiled. For so many years, the two of them rarely spoke about my sister, but lately, they talked more often, and things were comfortable between them. Mom had no reason to worry. He looked at her and their eyes held for a moment. It is okay, Dave. "You don't need a clever way to ask me." "I like seeing you happy." And I know you miss them. Dad said. "Thank you, Robert. Really! You don't know what it means to me." "I think I do," Dad said.

The Lord answered mom's prayer. Love without limits. The thought of my sister and her daughter returning I believe that something had changed, and it meant that our support had to be as real and reliable as much as our home. Over the next week, mom spent hours making new house arrangements. Each is detailed with house rules. My parents are kind, generous, and funny people, so living with them again in midlife must have been an exercise in patience and humor for my sister. That summer, we welcomed my sister and niece home. It was time. There was no explanation needed for their return. Mom knew it when she saw them getting off the plane and walking toward her that afternoon. No matter how far they had come, mom loved this part. Of course, dad and I felt the beginning of tears and blinked them back. Even when no one else understood, dad did. As we gathered, my niece turned and eased her way to me. We hugged for a 142-long moment. She drew back enough to see my face. "We are finally home. I'm good now." We walked and talked a little more as dad collected their luggage and made our way back to the car. Mom thanked God for her child and prayed that she would never leave again.

Mom had scheduled family day that following Sunday, and my sister was surprised at the response. She had been skeptical at first, but she had a rare smile that lit her face. At least one relative from each of our families attended. Best of all, one of her long-time friends came. She could have scolded her for not keeping in touch, but she didn't. Yet, she opened her arms and welcomed my sister home. We laughed and talked about memories of our childhood and how everything in life takes time.

One particular memory presented itself that morning. The day we laughed so hard as I stood in mom's flower bed covered in red fire ants! She stripped me butt-naked right where I stood. It was a miracle that I came out without a red welt or a sting. Mom said she *knew* I was covered in the Blood of Jesus. Praise God! I was amazed by how much had happened and time had passed. I'm not sure if we ever laughed that hard again.

The Bible says that accepting God's gift of redemption is the first step to real love. I will redeem you with an outstretched arm and mighty acts of judgment." (Exodus 6:6). There are always and forever obstacles in our paths. Everything was going exactly well, but I could tell as the days went by, the chances of my sister moving forward grew smaller and smaller. It was as if she found herself in a dark place with nothing to do, so I stayed as close as possible because I saw something had changed in her eyes, but it was too late for me. Several months passed, and she had gotten adjusted to her new life, found a house, and started a new job, but to me, something didn't feel right. She wasn't happy, and I could feel it.

My sister saw me sitting under our favorite family tree on a lazy Sunday evening. She gave me one of those patented teenage looks as if to say there's no way she and I descended from the same evolutionary chain. I leveled my gaze on her refusing to be bested but found myself staring. I almost asked, "How did you get here, but I realized did I want to hear the real answer?" Instead, I asked, "Sis, what's going on with you?" It's like you have a secret. She took a deep breath and stared at me carefully.

"You always knew how to light up a room." She said.

"Okay, listen, I'm only sharing this with you because I can trust you, and besides, you are still my 'Lil' brat." She told me she was diagnosed with Helicobacter pylori (peptic ulcers). A few years ago, she started having serious stomach problems and sharp stabs of pain from nowhere, paralyzing her for an hour or two. At first, it would happen once a week, but soon it started happening almost every other day. She got sick and wound up with an infection, but the medicine didn't work for some reason, and she got nerve damage. Which wasn't a big deal, but there were certain lifestyle issues she couldn't handle. She had no insurance at the time and decided to delay the repair. On top of this, her financial situation was getting out of hand. Her credit cards were maxed out from paying other bills to stay afloat. That's when she realized she had to return home. Her face crumpled. Hence. The big secret! It felt like a fist in my gut. "I love you, brat, but don't you feel sorry for me," she said. "I'm so sorry, sis," I said.

We took a moment to compose ourselves. The way I saw it, her story had to have a happy ending. Who wouldn't want that for their sibling? My sister did her best to prepare me, but I wasn't. It is so easy to presume that while your world has ground, someone else's has come to an absolute halt. I don't know how long it took my mother to wonder why we weren't coming to dinner as much.

My dad was so quiet that I wondered if the news would surprise him. He was always ready and comfortable with uncertainty, ambiguity, and change. Especially these days, that's an incredibly predominant skill he had. On the other hand, I hated being surprised. I love surprising others, but not myself. This particular illness had a poor prognosis, so I needed to think ahead to what would happen next.

My sister's appearance left me with a vague sense of unease, which sharpened my observation. Little by little, pieces of her started to dwindle. I can't stand the thought of losing her, either. I also wondered if my sister's sickness was an oversight or if I had been waiting for her to return so that I could grow up. I remember when I began praying specifically for her healing and for the Lord to remove the ulcers. God's answers to my prayers are not always yes. Sometimes it is no. There is some consolation in knowing that change, even difficult change, can bring out our personal and spiritual growth. Prayer is vital to our walk with Christ; you will find that we can bring anything to the Lord. He already knows our hearts, so what could we possibly say that He doesn't already know? You speak to God through prayer and listen to Him through prayer. When you pray, believe in your prayers and with the right motives for His will to be done.

Three days after I prayed this particular prayer, my dreams intensified. The first dream came while I was taking a nap after church. I see an IV fluid dripping fast into a central line. The saline pumps are inflated. As I watched, the silhouette was smooth, blurry, and obliterated until I saw a face that could have been anyone. I tried to reach for her, but she left. In my second dream, I am leaving the maternity ward. It was fairly light, although there were no windows and no apparent source of light. "This isn't my sister," I yelled. Each night after the dreams, I dread falling asleep, wondering if I will see death. I tied myself in knots thinking about it.

The Call

On Friday, May 23, 1997, it was about one in the morning, and this was the last night I would close my eyes for fear of what I might see, and it was the last night I wasn't in terror of what I might wake up too. I drifted off to sleep when I heard the phone ringing. I opened my eyes. Mom called. I got out of bed, pulled on all the clothes I could grab, and felt a rush of adrenaline that was not pleasant. I picked up my keys, grabbed my purse, and flew out the back door and into my car. I knew immediately that this was bigger than anything I could have imagined. I was driving as fast as I could. When I pulled up, I saw crowds of people in the headlights. Sirens and lights were flashing, and EMTs were walking toward the house. I could tell from the demeanor of one of the men that this was serious. They parted as I floated through them. I heard someone say, 'That's Toni!' When I stepped out of the car, my composure dissipated when I saw my mom. We stood by the front entrance to the house, and I started to cry in my mom's arms as my dad wrapped his arms around her. It's awful, cringe-worthy, but I sob as mom holds me, strokes my hair, and tells me, "Toni baby," She's gone!

For ten seconds, fifteen, and twenty, my breath is coming shorter and shorter until I'm holding it and not breathing at all. There's a coroner there. He stops speaking for a while. At this moment, in the direct aftermath of losing someone, there is so little anyone can say. Someone is asking him questions, but I can't hear it because the blood is roaring in my ears. I tried to get things straight in my head. I tried to piece it together from the memories, flashbacks, and dreams. I couldn't stop imagining her.

There was nothing that could have ever prepared me for the next week. Family members began arriving at our home early Saturday morning. There were mom's three sisters, two brothers, and Dad's aunt from South Carolina with her children and grandchildren. After that, other cousins, my niece, and her children were all arriving, all talking. Family members moved throughout the house, with many tear-stained eyes. Our house was full of reminders. How much my sister was loved and how much she would be missed. The house cleared as we left to ready ourselves for the service. Mom entered the room where I was, "Toni baby, it's time to go." Her face, blotchy from crying, peered around the corner. It took me every ounce of courage to stand up from that chair.

Although my heart contained gaping holes, I felt my knees weaken, and my eyes were on fire. I managed to look at my sister's picture the same way I once had. The same way I did when she tried to crack jokes or simply called me *Lil brat*. I gulped, "See you later, sissy."

What Now? (Part 2)

Because thou hast made the Lord, which is my refuge,
even the Most High, thy habitation;
(Psalm 91⁹)

After reading this verse about His habitation,
I walked into a place of solitude
just outside the hospital.

Why should I suffer from the same things if you are here and are my help? Why God? Why! God will meet you in your moment of greatest need. So if you have questions, ask away. After your questions; then listen. Just be prepared when God answers. Throughout our lives, we all reach points where we find ourselves wrestling with spiritual questions. If God was in control (as He was supposed to be), why did so many bad things happen? What if drawing close to God and developing genuine intimacy with Him requires you to bear something that feels unbearable? Often, when we want God to do something, the solution wouldn't require much of Him. He could give a quick nod. A spoken word. An answered prayer. In the grand scheme of things, just a small miracle. But as much as we think we know, the reality is this: we're not God and don't know what's best. God speaks through circumstances. And what's more, He invites our questions. He would rather have you yell and scream at Him than abandon your relationship with Him.

In fact, God welcomes your anguish and anger, and you don't have to stop there. If we become stronger in our faith, more committed to God, and more in love with Jesus, our faith will be tested. This kind of faith requires us to grow out of spiritual infancy into a richer, even more, maturing belief in a God who is infinitely wiser than us. There is a time for everything. For everything, there is a season. A time to break down and a time to build up. A time to weep and a time to laugh, a time to mourn, and a time to dance. (Ecclesiastes 3:1-4).

After a while, my thoughts drifted, and I considered my own life. "You're a smart girl, Elizabeth," but should you change your study habits, we will have to limit your course load until you can show an improved attendance record." I had missed so many classes this year. I figured that perhaps I did not need a college degree. I had not told my parents, but I planned to drop out of school because I had planned on writing and being done with it. It was best for me.

But my father's health had changed everything.

Even if the worst happens, God's grace is sufficient. But I still asked, "God, please, see about my dad. Please, you are my refuge. In the most desperate moments, God will sustain you. As I penned my thoughts, I felt that familiar fear gripping me. The best part about it is it didn't matter where I was. I believe God is with me. I could feel His love. Though I could never adequately describe it, God's presence was as real to me there as the sandwich I had just eaten in the cafeteria. But in the stillness of the despair, I knew I needed to face this. Earlier that morning, mom called. "Toni baby, you need to get to the hospital!" I'll never forget the fear in her voice.

Dad collapsed!

My soul dropped when I heard this. Panic choked out my ability to think. To make it worse, I found myself growing fearful. Not a heart-stopping, all-encompassing fear, but the kind of constant gnawing that creeps into your bones when you hear bad news or see something going awry. His supervisor said that my dad had possibly suffered an injury from a fall while unloading a truck. He was conscious and able to respond. They thought it may have been a stroke. When the EMT asked him to hold out his arms, he did not hold them at equal heights. I arrived just as the ambulance pulled into the emergency entrance. My first reaction was sheer panic. It broke my heart to see him lying in that hospital bed. He squeezed my hand and said, "aww-one-in-a-million. I'm alright, but take care of your mom." Questions lingered in the back of my mind. I have spent arrays considering the what-ifs and the *What Now?*

We all face a staggering array of what now. Some, what now are minor inconveniences while others have potentially life-altering repercussions. Without waiting another moment, I drew a quick breath and closed my eyes. Before the accident, we spent the day together taking my dog Taz to the veterinarian. Afterward, we stopped at McDonald's to get fries (his favorite). We joked. He was fine. He was in good spirits. There were no warning signs. Dad needed to have surgery immediately. By this time, I'd already asked about some surgical options. The look in mom's eyes was a look to say, no matter what was ahead of us; this too shall pass. Mom found it difficult to face dad every day especially when he was at his lowest, and she knew there was nothing she could say or do to help him. I felt hope so strong in my chest that it hurt.

But I will never forget the doctor's report; "Mrs. Ashley, your husband dislocated the third vertebrae bone at the base of his neck. It is pressing against the sporadic nerve in his spinal cord, which has caused a postoperative condition that will have him wear a Surgical Stabilization for six months to a year. An external semi-permanent fixation will provide the greatest stabilization to his head and cervical spine. It involves a graphite ring to his head with Titanium skull pins. This procedure is called a 'Halo.' There is no damage to the spinal cord, so the long-term prognosis is good, but it will be a tough and long rehab. There are multiple fractures in and around the joint with many bone fragments. It has to be cleaned out, and there is a chance he may have paralysis on his left side. Mrs. Ashley, your husband did suffer a light stroke. He will probably need additional surgeries and a long road ahead on this injury. We will provide him with the best care during his stay, but he will have to endure physical therapy through our rehabilitation services for the next three months."

After the physician explained how the Halo cervical Orthosis worked, I discussed the insurance details with his administrator. She was compassionate. During our conversation, my eyes filled with tears. She said, "Are you all right?" I got a grip and got the words, "I'm s-s-s-scared." She said, "How about having one of the other administrators call you?"

On our way home, I had all kinds of questions going through my head. Will this work? This 'halo' may not work for everyone; would it work for my dad? What if the procedure goes wrong and it paralyzes him for the rest of his life? When we got home, there was a message from the other administrator who works with spinal cord patients. He answered all my questions. The medical staff in the Spinal Unit could not have been more helpful; they were honest with us and kept us informed at all times, encouraging mom to assist with his care where appropriate. We became more confident in dad's care and needs during his hospital stay.

Just as the physician explained, the surgery lasted eight hours. A bone graft was taken from his hip and inserted between the vertebrae, and then steel rods and screws were placed. Leaving him with a halo ring attached to his head by four pins. One being above each eyebrow and one pin behind each ear. The pins were about one millimetre into the outer part of his skull. Metal posts attached to the halo ring were on the vest. The post kept his head and neck from moving, which would change his balance until he got used to it. The vest was made of plastic, and the inside was lined with soft fleecy cotton. Dad had a few complications after surgery and stayed in the hospital for eight days, and after that, he was released to the rehabilitation center for twenty-one days. Physical therapy was a challenge, given that he could not do the things he used to do, and because of the halo, we had to be prepared to care for all of his basic needs after he left rehabilitation.

In the meantime, I moved back home to help mom care for dad. We were facing at least twelve weeks of recovery time. Of course, the length varied from individual to individual. His only complaint was his head hurt. That was understandable. His right side was the weakest, as the doctor stated it would be. The weakness affected his legs, so he had to rely on a walker. I could feel his frustration, but every morning I would kiss my dad on the cheek. My eyes grew watery, "I love you, daddy." "You're so grown up now. I can't believe you are taking care of your old man." "I love you to one in a million."

Over the ensuing months, mom and I took on the role of physical therapists. We made sure dad walked for fifteen to twenty minutes every hour. We did that every day, and his recovery was going well. The idea of surgery, physical therapy, and strenuous doctor's appointments had caused anxiety and left him with many unanswered questions. Of course, we answered them as best as we could. And he asked every day! Mom made a schedule as we both took turns sleeping on the couch with baby monitors ensuring we could hear dad when he needed anything. I could barely sleep. My mind kept spinning.

Just a year ago, my dad was normal; now, seeing him like this is not easy. He still had many years left. Have you ever faced some tragedies that almost left you in shock? My dad never retired. He never had a chance to visit Hawaii. These were some of the things he planned on doing, yet none of the things he experienced because of a spinal cord injury. He detested cigarettes, and I never saw him drink anything stronger than a Miller Lite beer; I never once saw him drunk. He seemed to be able to hold his libations.

Cursing was not part of his dialogue. Dad was always there for Mom and me. He attended every softball and volleyball game I played and never complained or argued. Six months later, we learned that the first vertebra had begun to deteriorate in the lower part of his neck. That meant if it was not removed, it could paralyze him. After the second extraction from the halo, he could not fully recover. My mom was a wreck; she needed my father around. He was her everything. We laughed at all of his jokes. One is he didn't have to wait to get his crown *'halo'* because God gave it to him early. We didn't know dad was silently saying goodbye to us. Memories of him reading the story of Gideon flashed through my mind. He was not the same man I had known my whole life. He was an integral part of our family.

November 26, 1997, the day before Thanksgiving and exactly six months after my sister died, dad got his 'halo' crown. He died at the age of fifty-seven, way too young. Mom sobbed softly and struggled to speak. "Dear God, Toni baby, how on earth am I going to get through life without him?" I had no answers. I was too busy asking myself the same question. "Mom, God will help us get through it," I said. She sighed and wiped her eyes. How could he be gone, the man who shared so much of her life? How could she bury the one person who had always believed in her? There was nothing he would not have done for her, and now she would have to learn to live without him. Robert Ashley was handsome and intelligent, a Christian man with morals and a sense of humor. He had completely swept her off her feet. It felt good for her to remember those things. The corners of her mouth lifted as she remembered and began to smile. At week's end, we planned dad's service. We wanted to reflect on his amazing life and the things he loved most his faith, his family, jazz, sports, and gospel music.

The obšeques was beautiful. The sanctuary was adorned with flowers to fill a florist shop. The walls overflowed with people in dark colors —men and women. Bowing their heads in respect of a man we were there to celebrate. It was comforting to know how well respected and admired he was.

There is no specific right or wrong word to say, but it is usually the best thing when it comes from the heart. Dad's friends shared some of the most awe-inspiring, personal tributes and stories I will remember and cherish. We celebrated him. He lived a good life. I think my dad was pleased with what we did. After the funeral, I specifically remember crying in my bedroom for at least two hours. The tears would not stop. There was an ache in my chest. I lost weight. I cried myself to sleep more than I slept. Sometimes, I believe my tears of grief were a prayer of strength to help me even when there were no words. I lost my teacher, my protector, my comedian, my parent, and my hero. I was upset, hurt the first year, and trying to deal with the pain. The waves of depression manifested like a rollercoaster. I know what it feels like to lose a father. There are questions I may never be able to answer, but what I do know is; God allowed me to be here to share my story. Spiritual things must come first.

On Sunday morning, a few weeks after my father's death, mom and I attended a church service. For thirty-five minutes, the pastor droned on Jesus' lessons on serving others. In John 13:15, Jesus sets an example for us to follow. After washing His disciples' feet as an act of love, humility, and service, He encourages us to follow His lead and serve one another. Not once did the pastor refer to my father's death. The service had been a disappointment for my mom, I could tell. After all, she had belonged there for eighteen years. I guess grieving was a private matter for mom, something between her and God. We drove home in silence. Dad's death forced me to start learning things I could not have understood. The impact a father has on his children should always leave a legacy. To me, it's not an option. Ladies, that's why it is important who you marry because the man you choose should have a few similar characteristics to your father. All Scripture is inspired by God and profit table for teaching, reproof, correction, and training in righteousness; so that the man of God may be adequate, equipped for every good work. These are all the things necessary for being an adequate father. (2 Timothy 3:16-17)

Being his only daughter meant my destiny would lead me to become someone's wife. That's what we both believed. It meant a lot to me. There's a whole sermon in just that fact. I have noticed that girls who grow up in a fatherless environment are prone to be more vulnerable, and that is the first thing that attracts you to the enemy. You cannot put earthly things above spiritual things and expect to grow spiritually.

Dad's Armor

I remember my dad starting his day at 4 a.m. by reading the Word before dawn. This memory remained his routine even when he was in his mid-forties. I have endeavored to understand the fundamental truths revealed to me by my dad and feel convinced that there exists a divine power that can lift one from confusion, misery, melancholy, and failure to guide them to an authentic place. And once an individual severs his emotional and physical bondage, he or she is on the road to freedom, happiness, and peace of mind. Dad would talk about God as if he had a working partnership with Him. He would present his doubts to God as if He were standing nearby to dispose of them. I did wonder, though, if dad had a special connection to God. He was always grateful for whatever life had chosen to give him. He could convey complex spiritual concepts in simple, down-to-earth conversations with me. He once told me, in his own time, in his place, in what he is, and in the stage, he had reached good or bad; "Every human being is a specific element within the whole of the manifest divine Being. So why be afraid of difficulties, suffering, and problems? When troubles come, try to understand the relevance of your sufferings. Adversity always presents opportunities for introspection," I asked him. "Why don't you say this to the people who come to you for help and advice?" He looked straight into my eyes. Then he answered in a low, deep voice. His answer filled me with enthusiasm; "Whenever we find ourselves alone, as a natural reaction, we start looking for company. Whenever we are in trouble, we look for someone to help us. We always look to someone to show us the way out whenever we reach an impasse. Look to God!

Dad said this is the correct approach and it should always be followed. Understanding the difference between fear and vision will enable us to seek fulfillment in God, not man." Dad led by this example. Understanding this bought me great ease. It was the beginning of my life without him. Dad's death affected my life so much that I hardly knew where to start. Since that time, I've had to fight the spirit of depression and anger. The tears I shed help cleanse away my grief. I need my dad. I wish I could get one more hug of protection from Dad's Armor.

One-in-a-million

Grief is unlike something so far away, and you return to normal. It almost feels like you are in the water floating; all the waves that hit your body have a different feel. My dad was incredible and a blessing to my life. The Bible teaches us to love everyone, and I agree, but that was a bitter pill. In my junior year of college, I faked sick just to get out of class. I could not make myself get out of bed. My grief manifested into depression, and I needed help. I had a very good friend who understood me. When I called, she listened. If I cried, she listened. She told me about a grief support group at her church and suggested I attend. I am grateful that I did. It helped me tremendously.

Do not let anyone tell you not to seek counseling. Do not be ashamed to seek help. If someone had told me before my dad passed that I would feel like this, I would have laughed and thought they had lost their mind. With the help of that support group, I can talk about my dad without tearing up. I have made a lot of progress and have been working on confronting my grief and facing my pain.

Since therapy, I have changed so much. I can honestly say that I have not been stuck in a slow move of depression since 2007. It takes a lot of work. I will admit though sometimes there are days when depression tries to find a way and revert. I know now that I am an overcomer. The day of my dad's death will be carved in my mind eternally. Taking care of him gave me a more vital understanding and the importance of compassion and patience in ways I would never have imagined. His death has a thousand endings, and I thank God in my daily prayers for sending Robert to be a gift to me.

When life gives us such pain, we all need to allow ourselves to grieve. We are human, and there is only so much we can handle but embracing the pain is a part of the healing process. There will be moments in pain where we will feel like we're only making it every day by leaning on the Word to get through the day. I will say that while grieving, don't close people out. You must let people love you, hold you, wipe your tears away and care for you.

You shall find deep within you that there is an invincible summer during winter. And God will use that summer's heat to warm other people up for His glory and your moment to shine.

In our pain, we must surrender to God and let Him hold love and minister. If you let Him, when He's finished healing you, He will use you for greater things in the next season of your life. I sometimes think if I had all of the answers as to why God takes away and allows loss and puts us in the cleft of the rock. My answer is that we are in the cleft of the rock because He is with us and doing His most extenuating work.

When I think back, I appreciate my dad's role in shaping my life. He gave me biblical principles to follow. If our biological fathers would give all within his given power to take care of his children who are committed to him and plan for a better future for them, how much more would our Father in heaven provide for the future and care of these children? Therefore, our earthly father's responsibility is to care for what our heavenly Father has commanded (1 Timothy 5:8). Anyone can have children, but a real man must be a father. Robert was a phenomenal role model. There is no substitute. As I said, he was an incredible man of God. I will see him in heaven. See you in the morning, One-in-a-million. I'm doing the best I can, Daddy. *What Now?*

It Is Well with My Soul
by Horatio Spafford
When peace like a river attendeth my way
When sorrows like sea billows roll
Whatever my lot, Thou hast taught me to say
It is well. It is well with my soul
It is well with my soul
Though Satan should buffet, though trials should come
Let this blest assurance control
That Christ (yes, He has) has regarded my helpless estate
And has shed His own blood for my soul
It is well with my soul
And Lord, haste the day when my faith shall be the sight
The clouds are rolled back as a scroll
The trump shall resound, and the Lord shall descend
Even so, it is well with my soul!

CHAPTER 7

Blurred Vision

Thou shalt tread upon the lion and adder:
the young lion and the
dragon shalt thou trample under feet.
(Psalm 91^{13})

Do not think that the secret place is without challenges.
The good news is that although you are surrounded by lions and
snakes, as long as you abide in the secret place,
you will be able to tread and trample upon them without harm.

Now lions are bold. They meet you head-on, unplanned and unexpected, like the phone call you never wanted to get in the middle of the night. Lions roar. Snakes hiss or slither quietly through the grass until their prey gets close enough to attack, and then the deadly fangs of the adder strike. There is no warning with snakes, no roars, no footprints on the trail of your life. The snake simply strikes, and your heart is filled with terror. Like lions, certain difficulties confront you, making you cringe or feel like running when they hit you. The reality, however, is that there is no escape from some of the difficulties in our paths.

After losing my dad, I must admit I messed up quite a few times, and those times contributed to a pot of brokenness. Often, we walk down the path of uncertainty, trapped in our limited ability to only see our circumstances in the natural. Before we come to Christ *(for real)*, our hearts' eyes are clouded with cataracts blocking our vision. This blurredness was one of my most disquieting symptoms. I kept asking myself, where is God? It's easy to say that God seems absent at our greatest need. But then why does He seem to be present when, to put it quite frankly, we don't ask for Him?

A month after my dad's funeral I wiped tears from under my darkened, bloodshot eyes, I believe God cared about me. It was a while before I could talk about the loss of my dad, but I took comfort in thinking that at least things could get better. Through my father's eyes, I can see happiness and hope. I can remember the good times and the times when he was healthy and we laughed. I don't pretend to know the *what-ifs*.

Internally, I was struggling. I did not know which road to travel or which to ignore without my dad's guidance. In the natural I saw things crumbling all around me. No one ever told me that grief would feel like this. I'm in such a dark place. I dread the moments when the house is empty. I had the resilience of youth upon me which to fall when my grandfather died; for me there would be other love to find and no doubt in time to lose or be lost by.

Throughout this time, I was told that the most shameful thing that could happen to me would be to be reduced to tears in public. I was still weeping uncontrollably and worse, I could not do anything about it. Being ashamed was the course of my embarrassment.

It took me almost ten years to learn how to cry without feeling ashamed. People say that change is the only constant, but not for me. I had yet to learn that some human relationships end in pain. It is the price that our imperfection has allowed Satan to extract from us for the privilege of love, but our hearts have eyes.

Racked with the emotional pain of my grief, I returned to writing down my thoughts and reactions to them. My faith in the sufficiency of God's grace never wavered. But I had to refocus. Some nearsighted Christians will only be concerned with what is right before their eyes. Due to the giant-sized issues in our lives, sometimes we find it difficult to focus on how much bigger God is and His ability to help us overcome.

When we face difficulties or challenges in life, we learn two things: something about God and something about ourselves. I learned that the ability to see is critical to human existence. Of all the organs in the human body, the most awesome one to me is the eye. Hearing, tasting, feeling, and smelling are important senses, but the ability to see surpasses them all. If we are going to live with our spiritual eyes open and activate our faith to another level, we must first get our eyes examined! We can't see ourselves, others, and life in the clear light of truth. Natural abilities produce natural things. Spiritual gifts transmit spiritual things.

Can I ask you a question? Have you ever tried to walk in the light of anybody else? I have not. I never thought it worth my while to do so. I sometimes hear of wonderful new lights that have appeared, but I usually find they only arise from some crazy-brained individual with no light to spare. Then, I occasionally hear of others who give out a sort of phosphorescent light through their discoveries or the cogitations of their massive minds.

The Psalms remind us that we are the apple of God's eye. God will see us through our pain, fear, uncertainty, and loss. The tough things we face, whether opposition, hardship, accident, failure, tragedy, sickness, aging, loss, or death, are all very real. They can be severe and unremitting, but they are limited to this passing life. Outwardly, we're getting older every day. But inwardly, we're getting stronger day by day, every day. We're being renewed. Our physical strength fades, but our souls keep growing.

So we keep focusing and refocusing, asking God to show us our blind spots, praying that God would correct our vision. God, give me eyes to see. Does your spiritual prescription allow you to see with the glasses you're wearing? Blindness, of course, is a metaphor for the incapacity to see spiritual truth. You see, the thing about growing and maturing is that you see where you failed and say, "I wish I knew better." Those of you who have walked this same path, or are walking it, may find that you are not alone as you think. Yet, there are moments. When we come to Christ, we get a lens implant. Your physical eyes can be open but not recognize Him. You can see, but you can be spiritually blind.

How do we overcome or get healed from our "spiritual blindness?" Sometimes our blindness is because we have unbiblical expectations. We don't read and study the Scriptures. You can't understand the scriptures, the meaning of the cross, and resurrection apart from God's help. We go to church. We learn to read the Bible. We go to Sunday school. We listen to our pastor, Sunday school teachers, parents, sisters, brothers, and friends. And in listening to them, we hear God's voice and learn to follow the Jesus Way of Love. When do we fully recover from our "spiritual blindness?"

Unfortunately, we don't. It's a lifetime journey. When I look back over my spiritual journey, I am appalled by how spiritually blind I have been, especially when I thought I had it nailed down. We are all on a life-long spiritual journey. We will never, at least in our time on Earth, fully see God and Jesus and fully understand Jesus' Way of Love. We have all been challenged by Jesus and Mark's Gospel to realize that we, like the first disciples, must continue to stretch and grow spiritually throughout our life journey.

It will never be easy. We will never finish, but despite the challenges and confusion on our journey, we will be blessed if we continue to actively stretch ourselves and open our spiritual eyes so that we may continue to follow the Way of Jesus. People of God, we do not have all the answers. That's why we must not pretend to have insight into everything we do not know. We do not know how God will use suffering for good.

But we know we can trust in Him because the light shines in the darkness, and the darkness will never overcome it. Let us live in the light, as He is in the light, and cast aside the deeds of darkness. "For you were once in darkness, but now you are light in the Lord. Walk as children of light (for the fruit of the Spirit is in all goodness, righteousness, and truth), finding out what is acceptable to the Lord." (Ephesians 5:8) One of my greatest fears is that I asked myself, "What do I not see in me? What am I spiritually blind to right now? What don't I see?" For true believers, believing is seeing because we have consistently experienced His provision, protection, and steadfast love. Jesus came into the world as Light, the incarnate revelation of God the Father. Receiving Him as the Light through faith is the only escape from the consequences of the unrepentant sin of rejecting Him. He came not to condemn but to be the light and offer salvation to all who chose or chose to believe. Jesus said He would only reveal Himself to those who love Him and obey His commandments.

Friends, there is a lot of darkness in our world, but there is also light. There is a light in our darkness. And the darkness has never, will never, can never put it out. I believe in this infallible Word of God. I would like to encourage those of you who may feel troubled, worried, and tossed to and fro because of what some heretic or skeptic has said. Walk in the light of the Lord and be perfectly satisfied with the revelation He has given you in His Word. The Word of God has been tested and tried for many centuries. It has never been found wanting. Its' light has never been quenched. It shines, if possible, even more brightly today than it ever did before. Matthew 5:14-16 states, "You are the light of the world. A city on a hill cannot be hidden. Neither do people light a lamp and put it under a bowl. Instead, they put it on its stand. Giving light to everyone in the house. In the same way, let your light shine before men that they may see your good deeds and glorify your Father in heaven."

We do not physically see Him, but obediently walking with Him enhances our spiritual vision-enabling us to see and enjoy the result of His extraordinary power daily. The fact that believers are eternally secure in Him, though we have never physically seen Him, is undeniable proof that no one who places faith in Him is ever too far away from His loving care. The more your relationship matures and becomes more compliant, the more you trust the Lord to respond with your best interest and needs in mind. We can enjoy

His presence unhindered in our lives by continuing to walk in the light. I've been spiritually blind before and didn't have a clue. But now, God helps me see Him more each day.

Blurred spiritual eyesight puts eternal salvation in jeopardy. It is not enough to keep Jesus in view. We must keep Him in focus. If the eye is good, your whole body will be full of light. But if your eye is bad, your whole body will be full of darkness. Therefore, these verses go beyond being concerned with the person's nature but focus on the person's actions caused by such nature. These actions can be selfish, greedy, or generous and concerned about the welfare of others. Our morals and ethics come from the internal light in the heart. That light of darkness is based on where we store our treasure. Everyone, whether rich or poor, is in the process of storing treasure. It is where we hold that treasure that makes all the difference in the world.

There is no doubt that thousands of us have not known the will of God because we have not entered into this great blessing of seeing in the Spirit. God has things for us that are beneath the surface of the spoken word. He has truths for us that the natural ear cannot comprehend. There is an entirely new area of the Christian life awaiting that believer who will enlighten the spiritual eyes. Pray for the spiritual eyes of our family, friends, and loved ones to be open to God's Word's truth. Especially those who have "Blurred Vision."

CHAPTER 8

This Changes Everything

Girl! What's going on?
Truth is that we are mostly
not hearing the same message at all. Why?
Because everything we thought we understood
and could depend on will be shattered.

You can be saved. You can be filled with the indwelling of the Holy Spirit. You can love Jesus. You can read the Scriptures. You can experience God's grace in a thousand areas of your life. And yet, you still don't know who God is. Can I submit that; Satan is looking at who God protects? Not only is he looking at you, but he is studying you. The Christian walk is a very high level of discipline. It is not to be played with. You have to contend for your faith! Rising strong after a fall is how we cultivate wholeheartedness in our lives; it's the process that teaches us the most about who we are.

There was a major turning point in my life, where a testimony that transformed me never came easy. Did you know that God will turn your life into a theater for everyone to see while He's protecting you? Yes, your life will be a spectacle. When you have to take cover, your weakness shows, and that's when God exposes you to people desperately seeking to know what's going on in your life. Oh, but in the times of trouble, He shall hide you! I'm telling you, when you are on display, you have to use your words. You must be faithful to God, even when you don't understand.

For this reason, I believe I am right where I belong, and you are where you belong. God knows what He is doing. Sometimes struggles and hard work are what we need in our life. They strengthen us. They teach us courage. If God allowed us to go through our lives without obstacles, it would cripple us. We would not be as strong as we could have been. And we could never fly. When turbulence comes, all you can do is trust God! Once the turbulence is over, we happily forget what utterly dependent creatures we are. Many thoughts are consumed with ways to make our lives more comfortable. We buy books claiming to reveal the secrets of an easier life. We enlist therapy sessions or take medication to minimize the discomfort that life's turbulence brings.

Although we will never enjoy the turbulence of discomfort and suffering, God uses it to strip us of our vain self-reliance so He can guide us to a better, more secure destination. Trouble moves us to cast our every care on Him. And isn't it just like God to use that which causes so much discomfort to move us to a place of indescribable comfort in Him?

We don't have to like suffering to know that God is working through it to bring us safely to our destination, a place where we can be settled and strengthened with feet firmly planted on solid ground. Growth requires turbulence. We can avoid it entirely by not flying. But then, we wouldn't get anywhere. What if instead of running from adversity, we embraced it as part of God's process of moving us to a better place?

When God reveals His purposes and plans for you through the seasons of your life, remember that even if He has told you how you will ultimately serve Him, it doesn't mean that the fulfillment of that promise will happen in a straight line. Instead, you might feel like you are going in loop-de-loops and circles like you are wandering.

Joseph must have known what it felt like to wander in circles. His story reminds us that we cannot determine what God is up to by looking at our circumstances. Although you are not given a roadmap for your life, there are road markers to ensure you are walking in your gifting - love, and wisdom. Throughout the Word of God, we are instructed to get wisdom. It's not a choice. It's an instruction to build a house of wisdom in our minds.

Eventually, I lost interest in trying to control my life, to make things happen in a way I thought I wanted them to happen. Therefore, I began surrendering to the Holy Spirit and finding out what "He" wanted me to do. I discovered that it wasn't that different in the long run. Instead of figuring out what I wanted, setting goals, and trying to control what happened to me, I began practicing tuning in receptively to my intuition and acting on what He told me without always understanding why I was doing what I was doing. It was a feeling of letting go of control, surrendering, and allowing the Holy Spirit to be in charge.

If Joseph's trip from slavery to seeing his dreams materialize wasn't a straight line for him, why should we expect it to be for us? Because we are often uncomfortable with anything other than a straight line, we may become frustrated when our purpose doesn't unfold as planned. Therefore, we must remember not to define success simply as a destination or when we finally reach some "ultimate purpose." Instead, we must define success as a process as we obey God.

Sometimes, God blasts onto the stage of our lives by doing something so miraculous we can't deny His existence or His love for us. Then we can feel successful every day; while we wait on Him to fulfill His promises about our purpose. Joseph had no idea that before his dream would come true, he would experience plenty of disappointment and heartache. It might have been better if he had kept the dream to himself! Because we know that his story ends well, just like God revealed in Joseph's dream, we also know that Joseph's life wasn't about the destination. It was about the journey.

Several years ago, I had become so busy working at all church meetings and events, helping people who needed it, and trying to make everyone happy that I neglected the most important thing; my intimate walk with God. It's not that I stopped walking with Him. On the contrary, I couldn't make it through a day without Him. It's not that I stopped praying. I was praying more than ever about everyone else on the planet. But I didn't pray about my walk with Him.

It's not that I didn't read His Word. I read for hours as I did research in the scriptures for different projects I was working on and the Bible classes I was taking. But I didn't give God time to speak to me personally through it. I was busy doing good and neglected to do what was best. I became Martha instead of Mary without realizing it (Luke 10:38-42). I didn't take enough time for God or, for that matter, me. As a result, I became so depleted I couldn't go on. I felt like that eggshell as if I could be crushed with little outside pressure. I knew I needed more of God in my life; nothing on earth was more important than that.

There wasn't anything else that could satisfy the hunger I felt inside except more of His presence. And I realized how important it was to guard and protect my relationship with God in prayer. The way to avoid the kind of thing I experienced is to pray about every aspect of our life to keep us spiritually anchored and reminded of God's promises. It will keep us focused on God and who He made us to be. It will help us live God's way and not our own. It will lift our eyes from the temporal to the eternal and show us what is important. It will give us the ability to distinguish the truth from a lie. It will strengthen our faith and encourage us to believe in the impossible. It will enable us to become the women of God we long to be and believe we can be. Who among us doesn't need that? Have you experienced feelings of emptiness, frustration, or being unfulfilled? I, too, have felt all those things. The good news is that this is the way God wants you to feel.

God wants you to long for His presence. He wants you to find your fulfillment in Him and nothing else. He wants you to walk closely with Him. He wants you to increase in faith and knowledge of His Word. He wants you to put all your hopes and dreams in His hands and look to Him to meet your needs. He will open the storehouse of blessing upon your life when you do. That's because these things are His will for you. If you're like me, you don't want to live the kind of life where you barely hang on. You don't want to merely eke out an existence, find a way to cope with your misery, or just get by. You want to have the abundant life Jesus spoke of when He said, "I have come that they may have life and that they may have it more abundantly" (John 10:10).

None of us enjoy going around in circles, always passing through the same territory and coming back to the same problems, same frustrations, same mistakes, and same limitations. We don't want to become calloused, hard-hearted, bitter, unforgiving, impatient, hopeless, or unteachable. We don't want to end up with a negative attitude that says, "My situation will never be any different because it hasn't been any different for a long time." We want to break out of any self-defeating cycle of repeated patterns and habits and transcend ourselves, our limitations, and our circumstances.

We've all had times when we felt completely powerless in the face of our circumstances. We've proven to ourselves over and over that we don't have what it takes to attain any kind of permanent transformation in our lives. We know that our best efforts to change ourselves or our circumstances in significant or lasting ways never work. We recognize our need for power beyond and far greater than ourselves. But there is only one power in the world great enough to help us rise above ourselves and the difficult things we face. That is the power of God. We know He has given many promises for our lives, but if we don't know what these promises are, we can't get a clear perspective on our situation. Remember your weary nights? Remember your painful days?

I'm sure you want a deep, intimate, and loving relationship with God, like many other women and me. You wouldn't be reading this book if you didn't. You long for the closeness, the connection, the affirmation that who you are is good and desirable. But God is the only one who can always give all that to you. Your deepest needs and longings will only be met in an intimate relationship with Him.

No person will ever reach as deeply into you as God will. No one can ever know you as well or love you as much. That insatiable longing for more that you feel, the emptiness you want those closest to you to fill, is put there by God so that He can fill it. God wants us to want Him. And when we realize that it's Him that we want, we become free. We are free to identify the longings, loneliness, and emptiness inside us as our signal that we need to draw near to God with open arms and ask Him to fill us with more of Him. But this deep and intimate relationship with God that we all desire and can't live without doesn't just happen. It must be sought after, prayed for, nurtured, and treasured. And we must continually seek after, pray for, nurture, and treasure it.

Every day I praise God for this smile because there was a time when I didn't feel good enough. If I could be perfectly honest with you and the way I view myself plays a major part in the demon of low self-esteem! I was either too fat, not pretty enough, or feeling the need to be accepted by others and wanted their approval. Life will be good if we choose to do things God's way.

Although I knew I was 'different,' I still tried to hide the fact that I was prophetic. I didn't understand and thought people would think I was crazy. Seeking love, encouragement, applause, pats on the back, and accolades from others left me floundering on my own, and none of these things would ever matter if I didn't believe it. Whether or not you consider yourself qualified, you have the responsibility and privilege to lead people to Christ for salvation. Becoming a Christian is a lifelong process. You can't hide what's in your heart. Man can't do what God can. Dig deeper into His Word. Spend extra time fasting and praying. As His servants, He expects us to be living examples of His righteousness as His representatives, bringing the light of salvation to the lost. Do not allow the enemy to trick you out of your confession. The letter kills, but the spirit gives us life. (2 Corinthians 3:6)

God himself is life. We are God's workmanship, created in Christ Jesus to do good works, which God prepared us to do. When you have to take cover, your weakness shows, and God exposes you to people who shouldn't be in your business. In times of trouble, He shall hide me. I'm telling you, when you are on display, you have to use your words. You must be faithful to God, even when you don't understand. Our quality time with Jesus, no matter the length, broadens our spiritual knowledge and deepens our faith in Him to do the extraordinary. The more time we spend with the Lord, the more we learn to apply our faith to circumstances in our lives.

God has so much to speak into your life. But if you don't draw apart from the busyness of your day and spend time alone with Him in quietness and solitude, you will not hear it. Jesus Himself spent much time alone with God. Finding time alone to pray can be difficult, especially when the enemy of your soul doesn't want you to do that. If you make it a priority by setting a specific time to pray daily and perhaps writing in your calendar the way you would any other important dates, you'll see answers to your prayers like never before. God has promised to show us a way through our pain and confusion to a fulfilling and satisfying life. God does not lie. Life will be good if we choose to do things God's way. Knowing This Changes Everything!

CHAPTER 9

Broken Pieces

"It's one thing to know about God,
but it's quite another to know Him personally.
Intellectually, everything was fine.
I was shocked into silence.
"But how do I adjust?"

Mom and I grew much closer after my dad died. She lived less than ten miles away. I would visit every day, and if I couldn't stay, I made sure to call her. I was worried about my mom being able to handle her finances. My dad always took care of everything that had to do with money. I don't think mom had ever balanced the checkbook. Dad had taken care of his business and retained an attorney, so she wouldn't have to worry about it.

When I offered to help and take care of her bills, she'd say, "Toni baby, don't worry about it. I'm fine." And then she'd change the subject. She loved talking to me about her childhood and how she was overjoyed about the time she went back to school to get her high school diploma. She shared how reaching that milestone in her life was an indescribable feeling. She even mentioned how some family and friends tried to talk her out of it, saying things like, "she was too old to go back." Some turned their backs on her, but she was okay with it. I saw the hurt in her eyes as she reminisced; some of these were memories she didn't get a chance to revisit often.

Now, I understood why she was the way she was; a strong, independent, and hardworking woman. Doing whatever she had to do to make it and take care of her family. Knowing all of my mom's struggles and the obstacles she had to overcome, I looked at her like, "my God, I think I got it hard." The sacrifices she had to make. I don't have any children yet." I had absolutely no idea, and I am happy God gave us these times to talk with each other and allowed us to grow closer. I don't think I will ever meet another woman of faith who was as kind and generous as my mother.

Mom was a woman who understood suffering. At times, God allowed His anointing to overflow through her because, somehow, she had extra love, time, money, and energy. She always had enough for her children, grandchildren, sisters, brothers, and neighbors. I dare not leave out her church family and the patients she prayed for. It amazed me how she managed to have so much and never asked for anything in return. That's an image of her that I will carry with me for the rest of my life.

Critical Conversation

There's no book! But you live, and you learn. I suppose. How can I make decisions and plans for my future when the here and now is pressing? Mom's decline had been so gradual. So imperceptible that even her sisters started limiting their visits. The day she no longer recognized me was even more complex than I imagined. It's words that are so hard for mom. She's speaking: sometimes, in short spurts and phrases, she'll surprise me with a whole paragraph of thought. She gets frustrated easily, which in turn, frustrates me.

Compounded by the fact that mom will never return to work, this was a difficult journey. Beyond her body's physical decline, she carried a gloomy and dark mood upon her shoulders. Many friends I've known my entire life don't even bother to ask about Mom, ever. I get it; I've never been one to know what to say to people in times of uncertainty. It can be awkward and challenging to bring up and feel morbid and depressing, or as if you're rushing a parent to a place no one wants to go. No one wants to imagine, much less discuss, a time when the end of life decisions are necessary.

In her lifetime, mom must have impacted so many people's lives, and it was apparent. Mama Edna, often checked in to see how we're holding up. Whenever she called, I was pleased to hear from her. We would have an upbeat, rich and funny conversation. Sometimes she updated me on her thoughtful neighbors. I tried not to interrupt her; one of my terrible habits and she never interrupted me. Even though we rarely saw each other after my early years, she didn't ask personal questions and never asked why I didn't call or visit more.

So how does one start such conversation? Nevertheless, this conversation was different; honestly, I didn't know what to say. I asked God, "why was I tasked with such an exceedingly difficult task?" I wanted to be careful with my words and at the same time give her some hope. However, it's important to be clear when we talk about sickness. I said a simple prayer before informing her of mom's decline, because I needed to hear a mother's voice. As soon as I listened to her voice, my anxiety levels subsided. As a mother she already knew. "Hey Ma," I said. "Hey baby, how we doing?"

She first said, "I know this is hard for you, but you are going to get through this because we are praying for you." A gentle pause came before I said, "I'm concerned that mom will soon leave me all alone; I feel hopeless. She said, "Baby, don't cry. Your momma loves you and she would not want you like this. You are doing everything your mother has asked you to do and you keep doing it all as unto the Lord. I am here for you, and we will get through this." I could not stop the tears from flowing and my words did not come out right. "What do people do in these s-s-s-situations?" I asked. "We don't. God is in control." She said.

My mixed emotions; my hands shook, my heart and chest were pounding as the walls closed in. I am grateful to still have my godmother. She's been kind, and loving during this difficult time. Her faith in me is humbling and I honor her role in my life. She has been my most steadfast supporter. Her guidance and come-to-Jesus-type advice have given me the courage to get through this Critical Conversation.

It all happened so fast!

Broken Pieces

On a Tuesday afternoon, August 2000, Mom had the first stroke and I was scared to death. I heard a rushing sound in my ears and my heart thumped when I said the most profound thing I could think of, which was, "Oh, Jesus!" Then I leaned against the wall as the nurse told me in detail how my sixty-four-year-old mother was walking down an isle of a grocery store, when she fell and hit her head, had a stroke, likely it was a seizure and I cried for what seemed like an hour before she hung up.

An energetic woman, high strung about everything in life seemed to have a more relaxed attitude toward the simplest things. I was sad to know she had to stay in the hospital for so long, but I was happy she would get all the medical care she needed. The whole family system is thrown off when a parent's physical condition changes. My siblings and I had to adjust to a seismic shift away from things that 'used to be'. We all responded differently. Each one of us was going through our individual and emotional experience. It was challenging to figure out how to connect with and support each another. This event changed my entire family. Sickness, death, grief and life changes can make people act crazy and rock a family's center of balance.

Family is supposed to be there for each other. We are supposed to be in this together, providing mom with the best parental care possible. For many, their family has always been the weight that keeps them grounded and their beacon in the storm. Then there is fertile ground for all family misunderstandings, as each family member tries to deal with changing roles and the different dynamics of attitudes and emotions. The tension skyrocketed, and sorting out the details was also challenging. Everyone had different opinions layered with excuses, and we avoided answering relevant questions. For example, who would be the primary caregiver? Who would be responsible for doctor appointments? In which an appointment was scheduled for the next week. Someone had to be accountable for making medical decisions and what to expect after mom was released from the hospital.

These decisions were difficult to face; sometimes, one of my brothers became overbearing. He constantly challenged me and had unrealistic expectations that I couldn't meet. He repeatedly criticized me when I didn't call to relay information as promptly as he thought I should. In the heat of a moment, he would bring up old childhood memories I had buried years ago.

As often as momma and I had conversations on this topic, e.g., her health, she always said, "I know he will be the one to take care of me." I wished he had been more proactive with her and her health when he visited. He became 'the one' in her eyes because she believed he was a natural leader. It didn't matter to me so much as how he came to the role. What mattered was how he handled mom's business affairs and health needs. I placed his self-righteous indignation on a pedestal.

When we bought mom home, he didn't communicate with any of her doctors or attempt to research options for short-term care facilities. He was great with strategy and assertiveness, but he was not so good regarding emotional tasks and soft skills. I could tell by his actions that he couldn't handle being in the room with mom for very long. It's not the little time he spent with her but his lack of empathy. We all have different strengths and weaknesses, but this is our mother. Exactly two years after losing my dad, moving back into the caregiving role was more of an emotionally complicated adjustment.

But because of the Scripture, this prose verse came to my mind. I can do all things through Christ who strengthens me. (Philippians 4:13) There was no time to waste, so I took upon myself the task of cleaning up and beautifying mom's house in preparation for her return. Cleaning was no small task. Mom's house was always clean, but the bathroom needed an immediate update. The house started coming alive within a few days and looked nice.

Before she was released, mom began to experience some complications. The stroke had hampered her speech. She had paralysis in her left arm, hand and leg. There were a few nights we got to spend together, and each time I entered her room, I had to take a deep breath so that none of my worries would enter with me and I could be fully present with her. I had a small couch next to her bed where I would sleep. I didn't exactly sleep but was just there for her. I didn't want to fall asleep in case she needed me. We woke up the following day for her medical exams, and after she was bathed, I would read the 23rd Psalm to her. Mom was sick, which was obvious, but she managed enough to tell me she needed scripture and prayer.

My youngest brother and I assumed eighty-five percent of the responsibility of caregiving. During the day, we would listen to inspirational talks and watch TBN or the Word Network. We developed something of a routine and then waited for another day.

We both cared for mom in ways we never even managed for ourselves. We did things that we didn't know we could do. I gradually accepted the idea that mom might not recover from the stroke. I think she was going through the same process. One night, I often woke to check on her because she was in pain. That was the night I knew mom wouldn't be with us long. She looked lovingly at me and fell asleep that way. That image is burned in my memory.

In the early hours of August 18, Mom had the first of two seizure attacks. There was nothing I could do. My whole life with my mother flashed before my eyes, and I broke down. But then, it didn't occur to my brothers to open their eyes and see that we had entered a new chapter of mom's life - *the last one*. How did she know? How did she know this would be my lot? The one to make sure her last wishes were carried out?

Unfortunately, what happened next; was a bit of a mixed dream, a blur, and in some ways, a blessing. My brother came to visit mom on Labor Day. Strangely enough, when it came to the day before his visit, I saw nuance in mom's facial expressions. It was different. He had a strange look in his eyes, and he came with an attitude. I respected him, but it was obvious that he was stubborn, which showed in his demeanor. This time his stubbornness had crossed the line, which caused a weird feeling in the pit of my stomach. When an odd feeling hits you like this, it's called discernment. But the Bible commands that we are to be innocent as to what is evil (Rom. 16:19). Our efforts in discernment should revolve around knowing the truth so that we might see the evil in contrast to what is true. When we know what is true, we will more easily identify what is and who is in error.

Due to his repudiate help, whatever was in his heart that he had held back to say to me came out as: "It's your fault." Mom heard him and was highly disappointed that he uttered those words in her presence. His words hurt both of us deeply. I was utterly disenchanted, but I was relaxed and level-headed before I said, "Let me make this VERY clear and highlight these facts for you. I do not get paid for taking care of our mother! She doesn't qualify to have in-home support. I take her to every Drs. Appointment. I take care of her personal needs; cooking, cleaning, laundry, and shopping. I bath her every day. No help from you! You can come and go as you please, just to sit here with her for a couple of hours to say you have spent some time with her. Come on! Excuse me while I continue taking care of our mother." We didn't speak to each other for a while. I can't tell you that didn't worry me, but I had to push through my feelings and take care of mom.

Over the next several months, I faced more challenges with little time for me. Mom's first appointment with the neurologist was finally here. She had a positive attitude and didn't appear as nervous as I did. Magnetic resonance imaging (MRI) confirmed the worse. Mom had been suffering from carotid artery dissection (Ischemic strokes). After giving us the report, the doctor didn't sound encouraging at all about her being able to lead an everyday life.

He said, "The image showed a small tear in the wall of an artery that delivers blood from the heart to the brain (which probably occurred because of a car accident she had one year ago). Aphasia was the result of damage caused to the left side of her brain, which is the area that affected her speech and language." Mom's left side was still very weak. He said, "Some people with aphasia may not be able to understand written or spoken language, read, write, or express their thoughts, but some recover fully from a stroke, while others face challenges for the rest of their lives. Then there are people considered disabled and can no longer work."

I took a deep breath. Immediately following the doctor's diagnosis, I asked about her growing confusion. "Her memory may betray her more and more over time. If it does not pose any physical danger to her, just go along with her. Don't try to correct her or convince her otherwise. It will only upset her. "And try not to let her words hurt your feelings." He said. The best thing we could do was make mom comfortable, and because of her overall health, she didn't qualify for any treatment.

During our car ride home, she was silent. I looked over and asked, "Mom, what are you thinking? You've been quiet since the appointment?" "Toni baby, I don't want to go to another specialist. I'm tired of being sick. I know something is wrong with me, but I am going to be fine," She said. Now, what we will not do is give in to the enemy. You and I will continue to pray and trust God for His healing as we've always done." Now say AMEN!" She said. Through it all, her outlook remained positive. My spirit leaped as she touched me with the excitement of her determination. She was never embarrassed about having a stroke, and for this reason, she was my- Ŝĥĕřŏ.

As I continued to drive, tears welled in my eyes that I dared not let her see. I did not want to accept what was happening. No matter how much I cried, hoped, and prayed; it was *surreal*. Mom was still strong in her faith and the courage I always knew she had. All of her life, she was a fighter, even for her siblings. When things went wrong in their lives, she would encourage them in the best way she knew how and here it is; who would fight for her? I thought. I kept telling her every chance I'd get, "I'm right here, and I love you so much!"

106

I would take her to her appointments and run errands with her. Every day someone would come by the house and spend time with her. I was happy that she was able to enjoy this. They showered her with beautiful flowers, note cards, and long healing prayers. We laughed and watched movies. I can't forget how she would send me to town to get her different kinds of food, and she would take just a bite or two and feel full. But I would laugh because I just wanted to see her eat something. She would tell everybody who came by to bring her food and make me lie and say that she enjoyed the food. She could be funny and charming one minute and aggressively opinionated the next. We talked about many happy times. About a week before mom died, one of the last times she was awake, she took my hand and said, "Toni baby, promise me you will be good to your brothers, keep praying for them, check on them and call them; even if they don't call you." Darn it, I was trying to avoid this moment. "Of course, I will, Momma." It was what she needed to hear. And I meant it.

March 5th, 3:33 a.m.

I cannot compare thinking about losing my mother to any other loss I have experienced. I have lost other family members, but it's something about the fact that it's *mom*. Everyone knows that someday their parents will die. As children, we have our parents all of our existence until we are parentless. I must admit that I hadn't realized how much it meant to know that mom was always there to listen, give me advice, give me the tightest hug and assure me that everything was alright. My mother was such an *amazing* soul. The day after she died, I walked into her bedroom, grabbed her pillow, and smelled it. I held it so tight and just screamed. Everything I thought I had left in me, I cried-*out*.

We had my mom's funeral Saturday, March 10, 2001, and this would be my first opportunity to view my mother's body since she passed. As we neared the church, there was complete silence in the car. I looked out and saw the green awning and covered chairs. No parking spaces. Standing room only as family, friends, and loved ones gathered at the triumphal celebration. When the driver opened the door, my brother stepped towards me and extended his arm for support.

107

I accepted. We had spoken a few times leading up to mom's death, but I no longer held him on a pedestal. As we walked into the sanctuary, an usher handed me several tissues. I looked towards the altar and saw the light blue casket donned with white carnations; the family had picked out for her. She loved flowers. Mom once told me that carnations were her secret flower because they symbolize a *mother's love*. She specifically asked for white ones because they carry the thought of purity. We slowly walked down the aisle to see my mother for the last time. As I neared the casket, I couldn't say or do anything other than stare at my mom. I kept looking at her until I uttered, "Wake up! Wake up, please!" The tears poured down my face. I kissed her on the forehead. That was it.

This moment would be the last time I saw my mom's face. As I let the tears flow this time, it was accompanied by a huge, painful lump in my throat. A body full of life, wisdom, faith, strength, courage, compassion, and love was gone. I sat there looking at her knowing deep down inside I had to accept death. I don't have a choice. My mother was not coming back. The undertaker came up to the casket and began to close it, and tightening the top down was hard to watch. I couldn't even pay attention to what the pastor was saying; I continued staring at the casket surrounded by many beautiful flower arrangements.

Everything was a blur from that moment on. My siblings and I were the first to walk over to the grave. I remember sitting in front of the empty hole in the ground and watching my two older brothers, along with the pall bearers, carry the casket towards me and place it on the stand over the grave. The pastor came over and said a little prayer over my mom, and then my older brother spoke. I do not remember what he said that day, but I know I saw him break down as I had never before.

Once he finished speaking, it was that time. It was time to lower the casket to the ground. As they lowered my mother to the ground, I cried so hard all over again. The hardest thing I had to do was leave. I wasn't in a rush to go. I wanted to stay as long as I could until the workers came to seal the grave. I didn't know this would affect me so badly, but it did. I began crying so hard I started to get the uncontrollable twitches a child gets from crying.

I created a definitive mental wall of apathy to hide my depression. Everything had engulfed me. On the day of mom's service, the lights in my soul went dim. Naturally, my thoughts centered on her, wishing she could still be alive to continue praying for her children. But I know the Lord Jesus is always here, interceding on our behalf. I dream of my mother frequently, and in my dreams, she's alive, and nothing has changed, but sometimes I forget the pitch of her voice, but I do remember what she looked like, and it doesn't take that much effort to remember. At the end of her life, I know she was comforted by the love of God. By faith, she carried that love, giving her the hope and joy she needed in her last hour.

ÇÄÇḦË

As memories spring into my mind, I realize that was past and never will be again. Yet there is one thing I miss. I miss my mom's beautiful smile. It is just a memory; my mom will never be able to join me or even reminisce with me. I linger over photos of my mom. Even in those frozen moments, I could tell something was not right because she looked more than just old. Maybe it's the way her head is inclined or the certain limpness in her stance as if there was physical confusion. Mom was smiling. She knew where she was. She knew she was with family, with the people who loved her and whom she had loved her whole life fiercely. I might be driving down the road and thinking of something she may need from the store. Of course, that triggered days of shopping with her. Sometimes I can sit and think of things I wished I would have said and questions I wished I would have asked. I would dial her telephone number, the same number I dialed to speak to her for years, just to hear a disconnected message.

While some of us must suffer loss suddenly and then cope with the loss of conversation and contact, I thank God every day as he allowed me to be able to go through that stage very slowly. Every day, every hour, I started to realize my mother was gone. Memories of eating her home-cooked meals, watching television with her, hearing her laugh, and talking with her. The days I passed by a Dollar General store created an episode. It was hard, and now it is reality and a part of my life. I thank God that he allowed her to be in a good portion of my life. I often hear others talk of their moms, and I whisper, you better appreciate her while you have her. Life is precious. I know that internal searches have driven many external changes since my mother died, but I am not the same person I was before. It seems the internal changes for me are the hardest to explain. A new seriousness has emerged greater now than then and, for the most part, a new sense of my mortality. I mourned terribly when my daddy died, but I had none of those feelings when my mother died four years later. My mom and I bonded differently. I did not want to accept what was happening. I did the best I could for as long as I could. The link that held everything and everyone together was gone.

Mom would not want me to write about her death, let alone dwell on it. I know she would want me to write about her life because I knew both. So, I wanted to write about the life she lived. A blessed life, and I am convinced that Jesus, who had promised my mom, "I will never leave you nor forsake you." Father, you said that you will hold me close when my mother and father have left me. Please heal the hole in my heart. It is shattered. I need consolation that only you can give. I give my heart to you. It is in your hands. Father, I do not want any part of this. It hurts. I belong to you. Lord Jesus!

I desire to continue serving and sharing this Jesus in every way possible. He who lived died and continues to live through the ceaseless ages of eternity. He has promised to return quickly, receiving you and me unto Himself so that we may live in His home forever. Grief is no respect for a person. When it comes, there is hope for the griever when we understand what they are experiencing. The cycle of healing from grief often goes through an eight-step process. If you are experiencing any of these emotions, please know nothing is wrong with you. You are simply going through the process of grieving.

First, the initial shock of loss is the intense emotional impact that leaves you feeling paralyzed. When I realized what I had lost, it impacted me to the degree of how much I depended on my mother. I could not breathe. The enemy used guilt against me from all angles, characterized by second-guessing statements like "I could have done more" or "maybe I should have done something different." There was so much anger and hostility. I didn't pray for a while because I felt like asking, "Why did you do this to me?!" I'm all alone now.

110

All of my energy was depleted. I thought my life was at an end. I even had an "I couldn't care less attitude." I can't begin to tell you how the return of hope gradually came. Finally, I concluded that I would be able to cope and God would help me get through this. The point of reality! My Mom is not coming back. She left me here for a reason, and I had to figure out how to make the allotted adjustments and carry on with life.

We must remember that grief is not predictable, nor can it be categorized. Sometimes the stages of grief will seem to merge and overlap. Helping grieving people calls for sensitivity, tenderness, sympathy, and empathy. There must be a dependency on the Holy Spirit for guidance. Jesus tells us in Matthew 5:4 these encouraging words, Blessed are those who mourn, for they shall be comforted.

Each of us should be encouraged through this promise; that Our Lord has given us. There's nothing like death, which brings to bear both the urgency and patience that life requires. It is part of God's gift of awareness awakened by a mystery that intellect has not been able to solve, yet it takes prudence to navigate the time spent afterward. The unique dance between mourning and mission can often be challenging to catch, but if life is to continue, all of us must lean into the music, even as it may begin as a poem.

On life's journey, I have learned how to be still by my mom's absence and be actively inspired by all of her achievements. What she accomplished in sixty-five years is an encouraging model for me not to waste one moment of my living. Mom's death was like a phoenix moment for me. Out of the ashes! That's how mourning turns into the pursuit of an inheritance.

In all that, I am grateful that God gave me a chance to care for mom and close any open chapters. He allowed me to let her know how deeply I loved her; so that she could go in peace. I had always heard people talk about the pain associated with losing a Mother. Honestly, I heard them but didn't 'hear' them. When she left, my world stopped evolving. I was left with an existential brokenness when she received her eternal wholeness. I will allow all she (and my dad) have trained me to do to take the helm. Although my doctor says my heart is in 'excellent condition,' he could only be referring to the physical realm because an enormous piece of my heart is in heaven now. Mom took it with her!

Yes, I miss her every day God gives me breathe, but I know I will see her again. When you know you belong to God, you don't need to fear death; because you know that death is only the doorway to a new and eternal life.

It's been almost twenty years, and I still find my pillow wet sometimes because mom and I are talking, and I feel myself waking up. I fight to stay asleep, but she starts to fade as my teary eyes open, and I realize I am dreaming about her again. I know she was tired and had to leave, heaven bound for sure, so I'll try not to be selfish by wishing she was still with me. I'll just walk on knowing she will love and live through me. She's forever with me.

Do you know what that feels like to have a troubled soul? I do. Jesus certainly did. Jesus knew both extremes because he was human, just like you and me. But you, O Lord, can only mend my Broken Pieces.

If Roses Grow in Heaven
By Dolores M. Garcia
Dear Momma,
If roses grow in heaven,
Lord, please pick a bunch for me,
Place them in my Mother's arms
and tell her they're from me.
Tell her I love her and miss her,
and when she turns to smile,
place a kiss on her cheek
and hold her for a while.
Because remembering her is easy,
I do it every day,
but there's an ache within my heart
that will never go away.

*"You will always be included in everything I do.
Thank you for being a great mother."*

CHAPTER 10

Hidden Entrance

He shall call upon me, and I will answer him:
I will be with him in trouble;
I will deliver him and honor him.

What was the point of feeding my body; when my mind and heart
had been irreparably broken? But I was not fine, and I wanted
people to know this. *Momma!*

Rain falling, I was up heart racing like my thoughts, sweating to the point that I had nausea and the shakes. Every time I closed my eyes, it felt like someone was in my room. No one was there. Kept getting up, checking the locks, and spying out the window, my mind spinning like Wile E. Coyote and the Road Runner. I spent the darkest hours sitting in a chair. I cried for fifteen days straight. I didn't sleep much and never slept more than five hours at a time. After losing so many dear to my heart, the dark influences in my life hindered me from having a rightful relationship with God.

After thirteen months, I can report progress in my healing and acceptance, yet the pain still lingers. I still see her in my dreams. I miss her terribly, but I am truly blessed by each minute we spend together. With all my heart, I believe the love between a parent and child is the strongest. The bond is unbreakable. She taught me I must live, even if that means living with a hole in my heart. The first year was rough, really rough! If I wasn't going to counseling, I would move to Australia.

Every day is monumental. Every day there is hurt and a void like no other. Some life lessons come easily. They blow into our days like a tender breeze. Others come less gently, like getting run over by a steamroller. They beat and pound us and come hard as God molds us into His image. I wish I could say all the lessons the Lord has taught me have been like a gentle breeze, but they haven't. For example, a steamroller describes my experience dealing with relational conflict more accurately.

I share this because it is far too easy to stay stuck in simply describing and telling one's story repeatedly, which can be a way of holding on to grief about the past or holding on to a narrative that places blame on others. You don't create "don'ts" to destroy your joy but protect it. What you fight for is what you die for. The more we accept ourselves, the better prepared we are to take responsibility spiritually, emotionally, and physically in all areas of our lives.

Mom taught me that a God-fearing marriage must first have a foundation with someone just as concerned about you as they are about themselves. She said, "Love is about two people sharing the same rhythm. Finishing each other's sentences and saying things at the same time. Putting the other first and doing things together. Most importantly, have someone to trust and believe in you even when it comes to an unexpected life change." That's what I saw in my mom's eyes in how she looked at my dad. That's what I desired.

My dad was always concerned about my mom. He would call just to check on her, and they had this little funny laughter when they were together. It was real love. I could feel it. I am sure they had their moments, as all married couples do, but I do not remember when my brothers and I saw them fussing or fighting. Their conversations were private. We can get broken by love; unfortunately, it can happen with heartbreak.

In every failed relationship, there is a journey of strength. In every pain, there is eventual positivity as we turn our perspectives to the purpose rather than the ache. You love. And you love. And you are broken. I wish there was a code for love, a secret we could learn to save ourselves from pain. Let me speak into your life; "Don't you EVER allow anyone to do anything intrinsic to your worth, beliefs, or standards." Why? Because God said so! God is love, and He loves you when no one else will.

Everyone Wants to Be Happy

People will hurt us and let us down. And we will hurt people and let them down. We're all broken people, and some are more broken than others. I wish you weren't reading this, nodding your head, reliving all the painful moments of your past, and longing to undo some loves or relationships so that you won't feel that dull ache in your chest. But would you have settled for less if you hadn't gone through what you went through? Would you have learned to fight? Would you have let go and moved on from someone who's not right for you? If your heart hadn't been broken, would you have learned to heal or go out in search of love, real love, again? After finding the strength and courage I needed to walk through this journey of pain, God humbled me. I struggled with depression, loneliness, and isolation. I was stripped of my self-worth and dignity. I stood there embodying everything I was afraid of and stripped to shreds with every pretentious delusion of goodness while suffering under the pain of a man who mentally, emotionally, verbally, and physically abused me for one year and two months. Four hundred days. Sixty weeks. Ten thousand-two hundred and forty-eight hours. I didn't know my value. I had fallen in love with getting married rather than what love meant. Naïve.

When I Don't Get What I Want

Here was a man that had returned home from serving in the Marines. Everyone knew him as a devil-dog-big shot-talk of the town. He was not a handsome man and did not have any outstanding features. He had broad shoulders, medium framed, dark-skinned complexion, and he dressed nice. He was suave and arrogant, and although he was not what I called fine, he had a little going for himself. He pushed a BMW. Some women had placed a mark on him due to his popularity. Now, I liked his virility and some of his mannerism which allowed him to become a very high-strung and extremely driven young man. However, he did have the typical "napoleon complex." AND I don't even like short men. That alone was a red flag. Again, he was arrogant and a bit too confident.

Will you see the flags? It was not until he saw me with my dad that he asked about me. I didn't think he would have noticed me from a can of wet paint, even if I had been glowing in the dark. We eventually me the year I was from school for summer break. He extended his hand, but I did not respond. He was giggly and repeating his questions. He started out lying. He later confided that I made him nervous. That sure was another red flag.

Whatever the case, I sympathized with him and eventually fell for him. We grew close, and he started sharing personal thoughts with me. We had some interesting conversations and saw each other exclusively before long. I became aware of how he trusted me enough to share his vulnerabilities. He was an only child. He did not have the best father-son relationship, but they did have an understanding. His mother worked several jobs. So, the least I could do was be his friend. His thankfulness eventually turned to lust.

Interestingly, he did everything he could to make me feel comfortable. However, had I known about this whirlwind that was about to have a tumultuous and devastating end, I would have run, dropped, and rolled for cover without blinking my eyes. See, he was a fast talker, yet smooth and cunning. He did and said all the right things. He knew how to wine and dine me without the occasional flowers. People with an inability to trust usually experienced serious withdrawal, abuse, or cruelty in their early developmental years. Let me say it like it was; he did not deserve my heart, mind, or body. My momma often shared, "don't kiss no frog for a snake."

Anger is like cyanide. It slowly eats away your peace of mind and joy and affects your relationship with God and others. I never realized it's controlling power until I met someone suffering from so much anger that it has left them bitter and unable to function properly. Anger can ruin our lives if we don't grasp it. And until you can make what Jesus did for you greater than what someone else did to you, you will always stay stuck at that moment. For the most part, I do not condone violence of any kind. Being more embarrassing coming from a man. That is right, especially if it happens to be your husband. So often, we look to men to give us the fulfillment only God can give us.

I cannot think of another way to put it into words without putting sugar on it. He thought I was breakfast, lunch, and dinner. One day he struck me so hard as if I was one of his boys from around the block. Of course, I was afraid to tell anyone-let alone tell my brothers that I became a victim of domestic violence.

He threatened me not to. Out of embarrassment, how do you tell someone anything when you are scared while covering up the bruises with makeup concealer? A foolish woman I was. Do not bother asking about self-esteem; it left after I closed the windows of my heart and soul. How could I be so foolish to give a man total control over me and, with it, a license to intimidate my being a woman? One he did not love. May I ask you a question? How often do you turn to God when life is good and moving happily?

Why Is Trust So Hard

God was married to the nation of Israel, but she departed from him. Israel committed adultery. God had to give her a divorce. This marriage was a spiritual relationship, but God knows how it feels to have someone so close to you leave. God knows our hurt, and he feels our pain. God knows the hurt of brokenness, disagreement, and divorce. Listen; I want to encourage you right here. You have to feel this in your heart. If you have ever experienced divorce, please allow God time to heal you from the heart-wrenching experience and forgive your ex, but be open to the possibility of falling in love again if that is your heart's desire.

If your boyfriend, husband, or partner feels he should rule over you, that is the first indication of a red flag. God did not give the husband the right to treat his wife poorly. You can say what you want to say, but abuse of any kind is not an acceptable behavior of God. Abuse is all about control, Christian or not. This man made me feel subservient and trapped. He knew nothing about finances or how to balance a checkbook until I showed him. Once he learned the process, he decided to give me the amount of money he thought I should have since I was not contributing financially to the household. Instead of treating me like his wife, he treated me as if I was his servant. When he received his paycheck, I paid myself.

You see, even the Lord Himself shares His plans with you for the future. For I know the plans I have for you and not to harm you, plans to give you hope. (Jeremiah 29:11) Too often, I sat in silence, listening to this man reveals his thoughts, plans, hope, and dreams to me. Yes! I listened. It is something special about sharing your future with the person you love. Be careful of the person you take for granted! He even went as far as limiting my time while visiting my family. I had scales on my eyes, and he always made accusations that his abusive behavior was my fault. Taunting epithets like, you're so stupid. Lose some weight. You're too fat, and his favorite was; you never do anything right. Day by day, the signs of his verbal abuse became my reality. Until I appeared to be what he had accused me of becoming, he used words such as mass destruction, which damaged the most vital organ, *my heart.* I spent the last four months of a useless relationship listening to a man blame me for all our troubles. He never took responsibility for any of it.

Even when I did try to treat him with respect (well, most of the time), everything was always my fault. I tried even harder not to say and do things to him that he did to me, but after a while, it simply wore me down to the point that I could not function mentally. Some days and nights passed me by, but I remember one day I found myself sitting on the floor for hours and hours at a time, just staring out of the window, rocking back and forth from being under so

118

much mental strain. With a deep sigh, I begin talking to God again, "Are you here?" Please help me! Please show me the way.

Immediately, I came to the cessation to making this life-changing event. Suffering from depression, and my own family did not know it. I had become a person living under constant criticism, which changed my physical features. The smiles that once shined bright suddenly replaced with frowns; the head that once held high began to turn downward, and the light in my eyes had turned dim. I kept asking myself, 'why, why, why, did I let myself get this far? I felt nothing was wrong with praying to God and asking him to help me get a divorce in light of the emotional ties and bondage. This marriage had developed into somewhat of a way like a hostage and a captor movie. I began losing my sense of autonomy as his assertiveness increased to the degree of physical and psychological control to the point where I became increasingly isolated. Often perceiving myself as powerless and with no means of escape. But God! I was afraid that I did not find a way to move on. I was not the same person I used to be. I had become a mere shell.

Exhausted, helpless, hopeless, and unable to sleep, eat, or enjoy the time. The feeling of any type of abuse leaves you mentally and emotionally drained. Lord, you are my hiding place; I have no safe place, no shelter, nowhere I can hide. I have such a raging inside of me-screaming to be free, and I cannot hear your voice over this chaos. You are the Problem-Solver. Now all I can do is cry out to you and ask you to Help me! Help me, Jesus! The difficulty of striving for his love became a nightmare. Seemingly I was the one who cared and ended up being the one who was hurt the most. In my lifetime, even in my own family, I have seen empathetic men and women struggling to leave abusive relationships teamed with an impaired partner, whether it was because of sexual addiction, suffering from mental illness, alcohol, or drugs.

He had many problems. He never kept a steady job. To make me think he still had a job, he would leave early in the mornings and not come back until late in the evening, or to add insult to injury. He would stay away anywhere from three days to weeks at a time. Of course, when he did return, he would lie his way out and back into the house, trying to explain how he tried several times to call, but I did not answer. A liar! He owed everybody money. It puzzled me when he came with gifts to make up for his lost time, and out of fear and loneliness, I would take him back after he apologized. For a year, I started counting the times he said he loved me, but I soon grew weary of being with someone who did not love me. Instead, he failed and disappointed me. All the respect I carried for him left, and I no longer trusted his words. I wanted out.

At that thought, something welled up in my throat. The further along I got, the more the enemy tried to use his tactics and schemes to stop me. My eyes burned with tears as I could not believe how this situation would unfold. I thought all relationships and marriages were supposed to be honorable. I was unhappy, and I knew this was not love. Unfortunately, things began to get worse around the house; I began to have panic attacks. I had to face the issues in my life and face what part of the role I played. I do not know how far I had gone before I realized I was living a miserable life, but now *Game Over!*

Mistreatment Induced Betrayal

Before I knew it, two months collided into a year. The past sprouted legs and caught the present. Soon, the phone calls stopped for dinner and the movie. Did I forget to mention the entire gentleman's qualities? They left too. The flags were there. No matter how often I tried to reassure him that I was committed only to him, he did not care where we were. I was in a difficult situation. In public, he would make a scene. My damn nerves were wearing thin. He accused me of making eye contact with other men. Just crazy! Instead, I went through the red light. Although he had not hit me yet, that night, it finally happened. Now that I had a man in my life, I did not go out anymore, so I spent most of my time chatting about girl stuff. As I looked at the caller identification, he buzzed in on the other line. I did not answer fast enough for him after the third time. When I did, he yelled, "What took you so long"? Being sarcastic, I spoke, "How are you?" We had been arguing for weeks about my sarcasm. I did not care. I was thinking things through while he was away. He yelled, "You are probably on the phone with one of your side pieces." "I better not find out." I said, "If you only knew." I was making plans to escape. His tone changed when I asked where he was. He said, "tell her to hang up. I'm your man." When I looked up, he was standing at the door with a frown, teeth clenched together and his fist balled tight. Looking at him, I knew he was here for trouble.

As soon as I opened the door, he punched me. "Do not ever put me on hold." "Don't do what? You do not pay my bills. I have a right to talk to whoever I want to on my phone." He has nerves. Standing in my face and placing a demand. Do not come in here with this tonight. I am tired. I did not get all the words out when he slapped me across my face. You hit me. His handprint burned my face. No man had *ever* hit me. Not even my dad. I did not grow up in an environment where men hit women. I grew up knowing the only time a man put his hands on a woman was to caress and love her. "Get Out!" "Get Out! I needed something to defend myself. I glanced at the knife cradle. I snapped, grabbed the knife, and before I knew it, I sliced at his face missing. "I told you to get out of my house!" What part of that do you not understand? Pleading his case, "I'm sorry, I'm sorry," he halts and says the stupid words some women like to hear after being beaten. Baby, "I didn't mean to hit you." I screamed, "GET OUT!" Now!

He looked into my eyes and saw how serious I was, especially with the knife aiming to slice him again, and then he left. As soon as he exited the door, he started calling. Instead of turning the ringer off, I unplugged the phone. I did not want to hear his voice *anymore*. I did not have to put up with this. He put us here, and he went way past the line. I took a hot shower and let the water cascade over the sore place on my face, and I cried like a newborn baby needing her mother. Oh, how I needed my mom. I stepped into my king-sized bed and cried harder until I finally drifted off. Weeks passed by as he continued to apologize. He said he would never hit me again, and I wanted to believe him, but a part of me was still hurting. My heart and trust were gone. When you are blind by what you think is love, you will only see what your heart will let you see.

The life I was looking at was through clouded glass. He did not know how to love. He had no love. For that matter, he did not love himself. How could I expect him to love me if we ever decided to marry? Foolish girl! I remember the first time he said, "If I ever tried to leave him again, he would kill me." At this moment, I realized that he was mentally disturbed. That statement grasped

121

something inside of me. You do not mean that. Yes, I do. I know I cannot live without you, do not ever leave me. I need you.

The look in his eyes told me it was until death. Even after that, I still had plans to leave. A part of me wanted to believe he would change. Somehow, I kept telling myself that if I could just weather it, maybe he would change. There is an unseen benefit at the end of the tunnel. Some weeks went by without any arguments. All of a sudden, something would trigger him. His mood changes were quick, whether it was something I did or said or, for that matter, something I forgot to say. Something had to give. Suppose I cooked something he did not like. He threw it in the garbage. In the middle of the floor and tell me to clean it up. You all know, damned if I do and damned if I don't. Well, I did not! For that reason, the gates of hell flung open, and he hit me until he ran out of words. With each hit, I withdrew even more mentally and physically, which fueled his insecurities. I had had enough. I just wanted him to stop hitting me.

It Is Easy to Slip

Internally, I was pleading for someone to help me. No one took notice. What did I ever do to deserve this much? Why? The verbal and emotional abuse was too much for me to handle. Besides, he showed his anger with an outburst of temper tantrums. One minute he was sweet and gentle. The next, he acted like the Tasmanian devil. His words cut so deep. What was worst, a man who cheated on you or beat you for no reason? I was sick and tired of defending him and riding on this asymmetric rollercoaster ride, especially not knowing when it would stop. I meant that this would be the last time. The straw that broke the camel's back. I had never had a challenging relationship like this and didn't know how to handle it. His voice and words began to play in my head. For my sanity, I had to find the strength to walk out and never look back. Where would I go? My family did not know. At that moment, I did not know what else to do. I was missing something.

I prayed, asking God to help guide me in my decisions and give me the strength I needed to live my life according to His word and His plan. I asked God for His protection and to have mercy on me. I did not have anybody but God.

Either Way, You Will See

My mind was perplexed. My heart was deeply troubled, and I did not know what to do. Who is this stranger I let into my heart, into my home, into my family, and most of all, into my life? How did I get here? I innocently fell in love with the hopes of having a Christian marriage and starting a family until Disturbia wrecked my home and life. I was not expecting this to happen to me, especially with the devastation to follow. Several weeks before making his 'big' announcement, I noticed he became distant, one being that his behavior was odd, which made me think maybe he was going through a mid-life crisis. Although his fiery dart showed outwardly, nonetheless, it was not lethal.

Exactly seven months into two years of being in this relationship, he stood and shared with me that evening why he did not want to be in the relationship. He said I was just a 'trophy girl,' and he did not love me from the beginning. He said he felt sorry for me because I had lost my dad. He cheated me out of the one thing I thought was concrete in my life. Love! Instantly, I began to feel like I may never get another chance.

Silence erupted. I had a concrete mixer full of contradictory emotions, and I did not believe this one person could cause this much emotional pain and stir up the inside of me and walk away. I was getting sick to my stomach. He never looked up to see the lump in my throat. There I was, standing bleakly. A transparent demeanor to make him think I cared. I will admit, at times, I was extremely vulnerable, even naïve. However, I still believe there is a God who will help me. Little did I know I had begun taking gradual steps toward where I needed to go.

What do you do when the one man you think you love from the moment you met has betrayed your trust and is standing before you to tell you he does not want you anymore? I stood before him, holding back the river in my eyes; I looked at him square-faced and said, "I can show you better than I can tell you." Hell, I'm a survivor!

God will take care of me, and he will restore to me all of the years that the locust hath eaten, the cankerworms, the caterpillar, and the palmerworm, his great army which he sent among me. And I shall eat in plenty, and be satisfied, and praise the name of the Lord my

God that hath dealt wondrously with me, and I shall never be ashamed." He thought about what I said. No remorse, he asked, "Where is your God now?" I walked off, saying, "He's watching you, and you better watch your back." Either way, you will see!

Close the Door

The following Sunday, I had to make it to church. Well known for great singing, worship, and praising. Everybody came for something; I believe we all got what we asked for this Sunday. As I sat, something began to stir within me. I felt free. There was a sudden urge to praise. As I began to lift my hands, it felt like God was waiting for me to let Him know that I trusted him, including the things He was doing in my life. I had a clear conscience and knew everything would work out. I did not think anyone knew what I was going through. I've always been a private person. I kept my matters to myself. If God couldn't do it, no one could. My trust factor in certain people I was around was depleted. I tried to hide my emotions the best I could because I had been to hell. Yet, I needed God to speak a word and heal the knife and scar that cut so deep.

My pastor steadied herself as she gripped both sides of the pulpit. She is middle-aged and a fiery prophetess. She began speaking revelatory and in a high-pitched voice. She zeroed in on my pain, confusion, and the hearts of worshippers. She talked about sin, forgiveness, redemption, loneliness, despair, and depression that weigh so many people down. "All of us want to be loved," she said in her Alabama cadence as she approached the conclusion of her talk. All of us want somebody to love us. Well, I want to tell you that God loves you. He loves you so much that He gave us his Son to die on the cross for our sins. He loves you so much that He will come into your life, change the direction of your life and make you a new person, whoever you are. She paused. "Are you sure that you know Christ? There will come a moment in which the Spirit of God convicts you, calls you, and speaks to you about opening your heart and making certain of your relationship with God.

In addition, many of you here today are not sure. You would like to be sure. You would like to leave here this morning knowing that if you died on the way home, you would be ready to meet God." There was such peacefulness that came over my heart as she spoke. I know God loves me. It is something I have known but could not grasp because of the false love I thought I had with someone who didn't love me. I could feel the presence of the Holy Spirit moving as if Jesus was present Himself. Wondering if anyone else felt what I felt. My eyes closed when she began with exaltation. I began listening for the voice. A sure presence was heavy; I felt it as she approached the pew where I was sitting. Why did I open my eyes? She looked at me and spoke these words: *Elizabeth, "God told me to remind you; He who dwells in the secret place of the Highest shall abide under the shadow of the Almighty."* I screamed and fell on the altar! I felt the release in my soul. I knew God was speaking to me. I heard the Spirit say: *"Now, it's over."*

The burden I was carrying was heavy. I had to praise God for His protection. I had to thank Him. I could have lost my mind, but He did not let it be so. The battle was not mine. Understand now that God does not always deliver us instantaneously when we call on Him. Sometimes we will have to endure suffering for a little while and let patience have its perfect work in us. I thank God for giving me the strength I needed to let go. As His children, He knows the right time to bring us out. In certain instances, when you are led into freedom out of bondage, you may have to go back and revisit some of the old hurts, rejections, and disappointments that had you bound. I say this with confidence knowing there is a silver lining at the storm's end. The light began to shine on everything I prayed for before the storm. Listen, I was actively involved in many church functions, including the women's ministry I served as president.

Furthermore, I served as the publicity coordinator and adult Sunday school teacher. I was always doing something to keep myself busy. My granddaddy would say, "education is good, but getting wisdom comes from a deeper well." A new horizon had begun for me, or so I thought, excited about God mending the broken pieces in my life, restoring the hurt, and giving me back my joy along with everything that the cankerworms, the sifting worms, and the locust had stolen.

Spiritually, I found myself in a place of receiving all of it back. However, before I could move forward in ministry at this level of anointing, God said healing had to come forth. You do understand that this is part of the process to maturity. Otherwise, how will you minister to someone's hurt if you haven't been delivered from hurt?

You will get caught up if any kind of hindrance or stronghold is involved. Get delivered first! Apologizing is not about you, nor is forgiveness; it is about the other person. You will have to be the bigger person in any situation. You may even be blessed in your memory ministry for remembering and quoting all of the scriptures; however, it will not help if you can't walk in obedience to your Father.

In 2013, a friend invited me to a revival service. When we arrived, I could see and feel the presence of the Lord as it filled the sanctuary. In the spiritual realm, I saw people receiving deliverance, speaking in unknown languages, lying on the floor. Some were worshipping and praising as the speaker was giving his message. My friend looked at me and said, "I know you see something don't you?" All I could do was smile. As we entered the sanctuary, we could hear people shouting as the speaker expounded on the Word of God. An usher led us into the middle section of the sanctuary; there was a brief pause for me, and before we began to sit down, I heard the spirit of the Lord call my name. "Come forth, daughter." The moment I took my seat, the speaker pointed to me, "Come forth!" JESUS! I said. I had never seen or heard of the guest speaker.

Furthermore, I never attended this church, and there was no reason for me to question God's authority. I didn't hesitate. I went forward, and it felt like a ball of fire. I was subject to the Holy Spirit. The woman of God spoke into my ear. She said things that only God knew. Immediately, I could see a realm I had never seen before. Praise God! Now listen, even though you may have some awesome experiences to come forth, let me assure you, the anointing cost! Before the Spirit of the Lord released me, I was instructed to go back to five people in my life and apologize to them. It didn't matter if I did or did not do or say anything. I still needed deliverance. See, that's what's wrong now. You think you are fine because you feel high one day and then low the next. No, that's a spirit of confusion. God wants you to have peace before you start prophesying and speaking in people's lives. Before you get to the next spiritual dimension, you have no choice but to release everything that has you bound. Nothing should be holding you. You should be free! Where the spirit of the Lord is there is liberty (2 Corinthians 3:17).

God wants you free to feel only His presence. I speak release to you now in the Name of Jesus! Release the offense; release yourself from all of the hurt and pain. Not only did I believe God released me, but I believe He released other believers as well. How much are you willing to pay?

In that same deliverance, I received some divine instructions from God. Although I received detailed instructions, there was no way I could face the enemy without peace. And God did. He gave me the peace I needed for my next assignment. Now, I just told you, there is a price for this anointing. I can't tell you how I praised and cried, but I can tell you this: "Jesus is real." I know without a shadow of a doubt. If you need to forgive anyone, you must forgive them right now. Why? God forgave you when He cleaned you up, and you mean you can't ignore. No wonder David said, it is good that I was afflicted; I might learn thy statutes. (Psalm 119:71)

After the word was released, I received it and believed that God was moving on my behalf. The more I yielded, the stronger my prayer life got. As time moved on, God did show me the five people. The first person God revealed was my ex-husband.

All kinds of thoughts entered my mind. I was so prideful! I walked in disobedience for three months. I knew in my delivered soul that voice was not God. "I'm not going to see him," I said. I knew what he was going to say. I knew he would cuss me out and call me everything but a child of God. God, I can't face him. I know he will lie and say all of the above. What? "Lord, you want me to return to him; after all, he has done. Listen to me! On March 22, 2013, I was leaving church service when I heard the Holy Spirit say, "GO or ELSE!" I'll tell you what to say, you just go! I was rationalizing my thoughts. "What was I going to say to him?"

"Okay, Lord," but you mean to tell me, after eight years, here it is that I have to go back to a thief. He came into my life to destroy everything about me. Lord, he even tried to kill my character and still my dreams. Can I tell you this? Can you believe he started showing up unexpectedly with a bit of hope? I refused him repeatedly. That's when I realized it was over and I was determined he would never get another chance to control me. NEVER! I always felt uneasy around him, especially with his history of violence. Even in those freighting moments, God let me realize that I still had to confront him. I was determined to be obedient to God, and I didn't want to find myself years later going around this mountain again. But, I walked in disobedience for another month, tormented each day until I heard the voice again. "GO or ELSE!"

Nevertheless, I needed to look straight into his eyes and tell him, "I'm not scared of you." And so it was. The day of confrontation had come. As God had instructed, I went to see him. The community where he lived was small, and the entrance was accessible. A few gentlemen were standing near me as I parked, hoping no one was home. I relieved a deep sigh until one of the men noticed me a few houses down from where he lived. I didn't recognize him. His features weren't the same. His age was now definitely beginning to show with a bit of weight gain. Hesitantly, he began walking up to me with a smile and a look of expectancy on his face, but before he could get close enough to me, I stretched out my hand to shake his and said, "*It is well.*" I saw the pain in his eyes as he looked at me as if he had seen a ghost. When he noticed that I wasn't afraid, he started to cry. Silently, I began to pray and cover myself because he was a manipulator. He could charm the socks off of a snake if he had feet. As the manipulator he was, this could be one of the many tactics he'd use to convince me how sorry he was. I'd fall for it and take him back.

Believe me when I say this: it did not penetrate this time because the 'scales' had fallen off my eyes, and I could see him for who he was. In that Nano second, silence invaded the air between us during his brief crying session. (In the meantime, God and I are having a conversation in my head) As he wiped his tears away, I asked him if he was alright. Immediately, he began to apologize. First, acknowledging the fact that the divorce was his fault.

I choked, trying to retrieve the gum I was chewing. Jesus! I felt like I was being PUNK'D and looked around to see if someone else was standing with me to be a witness, but all I had were my angels. He was a man who I thought never would apologize for anything. Listen to what he said: "You are a good woman, but I messed up because I brought the hurt from my past into our marriage. I didn't know how to love you. I'm sorry for the things I put you through.

I'm sorry for all of the hurtful things I said and have done to bring harm to you. I never meant to hurt you. I have spent many nights praying that God would get you back and give me a second chance to love you the right way, but how wrong and selfish I was holding on to a thought. I was afraid that God wouldn't let me see you again. I loved you and always will, but I know we can't be together like I want. I know you are a woman of God, and I've always respected that part of you.

That's why it hurts me so bad to stand here and admit that I am sorry. Now, I can let you go (wiping tears away), so you can move on and live as I know you can. "Toni, you are a good woman and have a good heart. Nobody has to tell me; I know that for myself. I was the one who tried to make you into someone I wanted you to be, but I couldn't. Only God can. He said, Now I know you can see through anything, and you still have those 'eagle eyes.' After that, I Closed the Door.

I Made It Through

Our conversation ended nicely. He laughed and said, yeah, those 'foolish things' you used to tell me about. I didn't want him to get comfortable and feel like we were on the verge of dinner and a movie. So, with that, I thanked him for his time, but as I turned to leave, he asked, "Toni, will you pray for me?" Jesus! I looked at him and said, "I never stopped." And so it was the beginning of emotional forgiveness. As I stated before, forgiveness is not only for you. It's also for the other person. Release the offense, whatever it is! So you can go to your next level in God. When you allow the Holy Spirit to lead you, your emotions can still be painful. However, you can endure it because he is always there to strengthen you. You see, what the devil meant for evil, God turned it around for my good. (Genesis 50:19:21)

This man didn't know how to love me. Therefore, I could only receive what he could give. Much of what I thought was love until God began to show me His love. I was always the one who was disappointed with other people because I was looking for love in the wrong places. When I read 1 John 4:18, perfect love casts out all fear. God's love is perfect. All we have to do is accept it.

Most importantly, love yourself. Without the help of the Holy Spirit, there was absolutely no way I could have done this on my own, having to stand boldly and face that thing I feared the most when it came upon me. In that moment of my life I was forced to reevaluate my concepts of love and asked myself, did I forget to align myself with God, or did my thoughts produce a self-righteous mentality? God knew what he had called me to do. He was doing the work. I had to be truthful with myself. When I look back at that experience, it is the mark of someone who knows how it feels to be alone. I'm at peace!

This emotional disappointment was difficult. It was all part of God's plans, no matter how spiritual I became. When you trust in another person, it hinders your dependence on God. Out of the pain of this hurt, I had to allow God to take me through emotional healing and set me free from bitterness. Yes, bitterness! I was bitter. Not better. Bitter. We only see the negative when we're let down, left, abused, mistreated, and cheated on. Because we're devastated, we're shattered, we're reduced to nothing.

But these terrible moments are not the end. Do you know out of necessity contentment is revealed? Beyond the periods of loneliness, my heart began to accept that I was alone but not lonely. Heartbreak teaches you to heal. Can I be honest with you? Even in this failed relationship, I wasn't worthless!

I know my worth, and so do you because even in the lowest moments, we didn't lose—*we gain*. Do you know why? I'm glad you asked. Pain shows you how to be strong when everything around you crumbles. Believe it or not, losing the wrong person encourages you to seek new love, real love, with the right person. I have finally reached a place in my life where I enjoy my own company. Yes, that's right. I was going places on my own and cooking a full-course meal and setting the dinner table with fine china for myself to enjoy afterward!

Though, I am reminded to let every present moment be enough in the stillness. At that moment, I asked God not to send me another man unless that man would draw me closer to Him. I was not negotiating. Timing is everything. God may be using this time of closed doors to prepare you for what is to come. It may be because He is protecting you. If God allowed me to stay with him, maybe I wouldn't be where I am today. An adjustment requires patience with yourself, your heart, and your emotions; even when the heart wishes and longs, you must keep moving forward. Adjustments also house pain. Attempting to accept the new "normal" is a source of hurtful awakening. Memories, at this place, provide little comfort for the buffeting. They bring back what we wish could be our current reality, but it's our mind's closest shadow of better days. I'm finding that adjustment also brings promise because it says that while it may hurt, I will move forward.

Sadly, feeling unloved is painful, but the pain of recovery is far greater than the pain of injury. After experiencing so much heartache and pain, I had to allow God to restore me. It is not easy when going through trails of any kind, and it's painful. From this experience, I realized I was at my turning point and believed God was moving in my life. For one thing, I was moving forward. I move forward with a tear here and a smile there, memories in tow. In hindsight, what I went through redirected me to God, but through this Hidden Entrance.

If you are a victim of Domestic Violence - Help is available!
Speak with someone today! National Domestic Violence Hotline 800-799-7233

CHAPTER 11

Beauty for Ashes

*"He has sent me to comfort all who mourn,
and provide for those who grieve in Zion
to bestow on them a crown of beauty instead of ashes.
The oil of joy instead of mourning,
and a garment of praise
instead of a spirit of despair."*

"I don't like to tell anyone about the things I've gone through. I don't want them to feel sorry for me or think differently about me. It's easier to keep my past to myself. Thinking about being blamed or judged for my past causes me to lose my breath."

Blue skies, rainbows, tender mercies, and silver linings. Whatever you call them, they can help you get through dark and difficult times. Blue skies and tender mercies are my preferred terms. The idea of searching for the happy little moments in life, and expressing gratitude for those moments, while we are also enduring the hardest of trials, is something simple yet can have an extraordinary impact on how we come through a difficult journey.

Looking forward to blue skies, journaling them, and remembering them has helped me get through some of my life's most challenging and painful times. I'm a recovering victim of domestic violence, infidelity, and trauma. Crying and pleading with God each day, I felt forgotten, unseen, and unloved by the One who promised never to leave me. Until the night I had a dream that changed everything. I was curled up on my couch in the dream, hoping sleep might wash away my pain. Tears poured down my face with sobs of sorrow. I was utterly broken, spent, and at the end of my rope. My waking emotions played out in my sleeping subconscious. Then, through the blurring of tears in my eyes, I noticed a figure entering the room. I knew it was Jesus. Rather than fear, a strange sense of peace, calm, and safety washed over me. He spoke softly and gently, with a deep, tender, and loving voice, and said, "Elizabeth, why didn't you come to me earlier? I will restore all that has been lost and broken."

Hearing His voice startled me into consciousness. I abruptly awoke, staring into the blackness of the night, fully believing I had just experienced a divine, supernatural encounter. I will restore all that has been lost and broken, echoed over and over in my mind. Comforting words I had longed to hear planted a whisper of hope in my soul. Words that reaffirmed He did see me, and I wasn't forgotten or unloved. Words that reassured me He not only had the power to restore all that had been taken from my life, but He indeed had plans for it. As a tear dripped onto my pillow, the story of Job came to mind. Job's restoration gave me hope, but as I thought back to my dream, I couldn't help wondering about the first question I had heard: "Why didn't you come to me sooner?" I honestly believed I had gone to Jesus. A million times. But I had not gone to Him with total surrender and trust.

Instead of surrendering my problems to Him, I had been telling Him about them constantly, worrying incessantly, then trying to solve them on my own. Rather than trusting for miraculous provision, I doubted whether He would come through and whether restoration was gone. I thought I had lost my peace. Yet, over time, I learned total surrender and unwavering faithfulness in God's sovereignty will always open the door for His restoration to begin.

Divorce can steal a lot from us, but it doesn't have to steal our peace and joy. Whether it's hearts, finances, relationships, or lives that need mending, God always has the plan to heal and restore. I'm still healing in some ways, but I do believe in transparency. Therefore, I know from experience that sharing my dark place allows light to seep in. Some stories are ugly and sometimes cause discomfort to those who hear them. That's okay. I believe talking, sharing, and having an open dialogue is healing.

Healing is one of those things that you won't quite know you need until you are faced with a situation that draws out those emotions from the past. My greatest desire is to help lift others in any way I can, and I believe that by sharing my story, I can lift others where they are. At least, that is my hope. God does what it takes to get our attention.

Beauty for ashes is a person who has a deep sense of failure, so many mistakes, the same mistake so many times, the addiction that can't be broken, is given a new sense of forgiveness, self-worth, and value that they find so exciting; life is transformed. Someone is wrestling with the hardest days of their lives. They feel forgotten, they've lost their job, someone has died, a relationship has broken down, and life is at rock bottom. Ashes discover that Jesus loves them, that other people love them and care for them too; they are loved; life is transformed. There are many ways these words can touch our lives, so many examples of life at its worst and how God can transform these lives by the grace of Jesus! The sad part is that we often don't see that grace; we get stuck in the ashes and can't see how God has saved, rescued, and graced us.

Over a year ago, I received a mail note from someone I don't even know. On a crudely trimmed piece of paper were these words by Chuck Swindoll: "You who have endured the stinging experiences make the choicest counselors God can use." I framed that quote, and it is in my office where every day I can be reminded that the 'stinging experiences' only make me more valuable to the One I long to serve. A heart for God must be broken before it beats for Him. If you long to be used and wonder why others seem to be God's chosen instruments, maybe you need to stop and consider how you have responded to the 'stinging experiences.' Do you fight them? Have you allowed them to make you bitter? Do you feel life is unfair? If so, you are undoubtedly sitting on the sidelines of ministry. But if you have embraced your struggles as friends and your trials as trainers, you know the joy of a deepening ministry. You can take comfort in the fact that the suffering lasts only a little while before the God of all Grace Himself will restore you and make you strong and steadfast!

The thing is, I never looked for ministry or sought a place to minister. I followed the progressive revelation of God's Will in my life. Beauty for ashes represents God's redemptive power from the very beginning. Throughout Scripture, ashes signify our human condition. Ashes remind us that trials produce humility, and sacrifices can bring about renewal. But it applies to those who mourn and yet waits patiently on the Lord.

Isaiah writes about people who need to change or be changed! There are many situations in which they find themselves, described by lots of different pictures, that show how they need transformation, but they can't do it for themselves. What God offers is not just a temporary little spark of encouragement. It's a complete transformation! The same God that conquered the grave can turn your hopelessness into hope. He drowned out the roaring lies spoken to me about my worth and identity by gently whispering His truths into my broken life. I have filled journal after journal with His abundant blessings.

My shattered heart has been mended, and my mourning has turned to dance. Yes, the best of God's people must sometimes sit down among the ashes and cry, "Woe is me." Indeed, some of God's best servants have been most often through the furnace and have been so long in the heat that strength fails them and hope well-nigh expires.

Even when you can't see how good will ever come, even when things are entirely unfair, even when you feel broken beyond repair when you bring Him ashes. He gives you a crown of beauty.

When you bring Him your mourning, He gives you abounding joy. When you offer Him the pieces of your shattered heart, He gives you a garment of praise. In condescending compassion, He took our ashes upon Himself. Ah, how they once covered His sacred head and marred His beauty! He took our mourning. Alas, how it made Him the man of sorrows on the day of His humiliation! He took our spirit of heaviness, and as He lay prone in the garden beneath the load, He was exceeding heavy and sorrowful even unto death. He took a loss to give us a gain, so it is barter in which there is a double profit on our side. We lose a loss, and the gain is pure gain.

From our Lord, the blessings of love are free grace; therefore, let Him have all the praise. When the Lord makes His people beautiful, they are a delight even to God Himself, for the Lord rejoices in His works and His works of grace-works are the noblest labor of His hands and as being fullest of grace is most graceful.

As I see the woman I am today, I get emotional just thinking about how I was able to excel in Christ despite the opposition I have faced. I can only imagine how proud my Mom would have been if she could see me now. My trials have literally propelled me into the Kingdom of God. I chose to stay in Christ no matter what. The Lord delights in His people to bestow on them a crown of Beauty instead of Ashes.

CHAPTER 12

Table for '2'

God keeps His promises!
A man whose love for God is the heartbeat of all he does
And all he says. I thank God that you are that kind of man.
I pray that our days together will always be the light
they are today, and I will continue to follow your lead.

Destiny is not a mystery. Destiny is a decision. It is a difficult
decision. A daring decision and a counterintuitive decision.
You fulfill your destiny one opportunity at a time.
Fast forward ten years later.

God's time has blessed me with a terrific new husband, Willie. I have a best friend! An incredible man who faithfully honors our marriage. Heaven stepped in, and we've been happily married for over five years. I still can't believe it sometimes. He likes me, and he loves me. I prayed for kindness, but he is that and a million things more. He supports me in everything. He keeps me safe, my head, and my heart. We laugh together, but it's not the kind of laughter where someone's feelings end up hurt. It's the kind that makes you feel more loved and in love and more grateful for the kind of love that brings joy to your heart. There's a lightness. He's full of light, and he shares it. He lifts, cheers, brightens, compliments, listens, motivates, and inspires me. And I do the same for him. He's like the teammate I never knew I always wanted. There is no keeping score when there's support and love. A supportive team is always a winning team.

God eventually healed my broken heart, spirit, and body, but not how I thought He would. Sometimes, the prayers we think He doesn't answer become gifts far beyond what we want or think we need. God did not answer my prayers all those years ago in the way that I thought He would or in a way I was convinced at the time that I wanted. Nor did He answer them according to my understanding of His promises in the Bible. And I learned that I could spend a lifetime trying to interpret His promises and still fall short. But I have another choice I can trust Him, even when the answer is not what I want to hear.

(Disclaimer: Before I begin, I want to point out that everyone may not know beforehand who their spouse is; God does it differently for people. Everyone may not hear an audible voice, and everyone may not have a dream (s)).

The latter is my story.

During my car ride home, I turned on the radio and tuned to a local radio station. A lady was speaking on a live radio program. She repeatedly replied, "Just throw it away and receive what God has for you." I pressed my ear in closer. "God, are you talking to me?" We can hear from the Lord, were taught, if we tune in and listen closely. Well, I was the one in for the shock. The following day those words would not leave my thoughts. "Just throw it away and receive what God has for you."

One day it hit me. Throw away "my list!" Yes, I wrote a list to God of what I wanted in a husband. My desire to marry a particular man was so important to me. If you are like me, we want our stories to be linear and laid out, God-like insurance policies guarding our biggest decision yet. But like our deepest longings and desires, it can carry us to heights in God when we allow Him to be in charge of it. Then and only then do we stop looking for similarities or common interests; instead, we look for that one 'yes.' Details inside. I spent a year in preparation. As I walked through that year in faith, I knew something was getting ready to happen. But then the end of another year came.

In my confusion and hurt, I searched for a conclusion-any conclusion. I couldn't understand why I felt so ready for a committed relationship, yet it wasn't happening. I realized my story would have a purpose; if I had not gone through these trials, you would not be reading this book. I believe with all of my heart, God still speaks. I believe that we can hear Him in a million different ways, His voice becoming familiar and comforting as He guides us gently. But I'm not sure God tells us who to marry before we get there, not specifically anyway. And if He does, I wonder if it may be the exception rather than the rule.

In scripture, God tells many people to do specific things, but he usually clarifies himself. Bushes talk, and so do donkeys. A voice comes down from heaven. God isn't shy about making his will known to us. But I can't think of many instances where he told the woman who she was going to marry, or even rare, told her friends first. Also, in scripture, God has laid out a million guidelines (a little exaggeration for me) for handling our marriages. He teaches us to honor each other, showing us what the other person needs and how to love and respect them best.

Marriage is an earthly representation of His relationship with us. It's safe to say He's invested. But I don't know if He plays matchmaker beforehand like we expect Him to reveal things to us like a Godly game of Wheel of Fortune. I think God gives us a choice. 'You will marry him, have three children, and live in a mansion.' There are a lot of bad options, certainly! And when we think about it, God doesn't force us to love Him, so it wouldn't make sense for Him to force us to love each other. He lives in us, His spirit as our ever-present counselor, and I think He trusts us to make our own decision.

I pray that we let go of our desire for insurance and reassurance and let ourselves get caught up in other things. I pray you don't see it coming when you meet the person God has for you. It certainly caught me by surprise. I hope that it takes you by surprise! When it's time for you to marry, I pray you choose someone because they want to marry you too! Not because someone forced them. I pray that you'll be in love with your best friend! It's not over yet. This prayer is just the beginning.

"Yes" of Love

At first, I didn't understand what was before me. However, the more I fasted and spent time with God, the more I understood. It took me about a month to put it all together. The turning point came when He showed me this vision: I saw a tall man holding my left hand as he placed a beautiful wedding ring on my finger. The problem was I couldn't see his face. "That's your husband; I thought I heard." "God, are you sure?!" That's him! "You are going to marry that man." My heart was pounding for the unknown future that lay ahead. It was an unknown future with no name attached.

My tears covered my pillow for weeks on end. Not because I was sad, but because it was a Promise! Not a burden. I knew what I heard. And I believed in God. The glimpse stayed with me for a while, but I put it on the shelf. If it is of God, He will bring it to the past. Even though I was excited, I didn't share it with any of my friends. I knew they would have different opinions about what God showed me. At this time, I was surrounded by women who, at one point or another, had received a false positive about who they would marry. A word, a sign, or an answered prayer would have left them sure- but then heartbroken because it wasn't of God. Esther was not unveiled until it was her time, and everything she needed was provided. Esther waited. My question to you is; can you wait?

When walking in the flesh, we cannot handle marriage's challenges (or the blessings). God's timing is crucial. The Bible is very intentional with its words. When you acknowledge God as Lord over your life, you give Him authority to rule over every area. Nothing is off-limits. Although God said everything about His creation was good, everything except that man was alone. In other words, in some situations, two are better than one. This scripture was the case with Adam. God said it was not good for Adam to be alone and remain single. What kind of companion did Adam need? Someone who understood his humanness. Someone who communicated. Someone who had felt like he did. I believe Adam was smart enough to know he could not have a meaningful conversation with any of these animals. He wanted someone just like himself.

You read the story: "And the Lord God caused a deep sleep to fall on Adam, and he slept, and He took one of his ribs and closed up the flesh in its place. Then the rib which the Lord God had taken from man He made into a woman, and He brought her to the man." (Genesis 2:21-22) Did you notice that God brought the woman to the man? If you did, it would make for a much easier time when it comes to dating and singleness. The Lord knew what Adam needed, and the woman fulfilled all his desires. I think it is safe to say that Adam was pleased with the woman God brought him. Therefore, I asked for a specific type of man and had no interest in switching up my preference.

Little by little, I looked for more Christ-like things I valued most in a man. I open my eyes and my heart to the possibility of dating. With that, I threw away the list in my head and also the one I wrote on paper. Being honest with God and letting Him know I would not be happy with any man. It would have to be the one He saw fit for me. The heart is deceitful above all things and desperately wicked: who can know it? To receive who God had for me, I had to know what to look for. Therefore, Ephesians 1:17-23 became my prayer. This prayer is for spiritual wisdom and will be the foundation of everything in your life. Apostle Paul even prayed this prayer over the believers at Ephesus. I was led to pray that God would give me and my future husband the Spirit of wisdom and revelation. I prayed that we grow in God's Word and in the right relationship.

I prayed that everything God puts our hands to do prospers and several other decrees as the spirit led me to pray. It may be different for you because God only knows the areas of your exact need and your future mate before you both come together. If you are not married yet, the best preparation you will ever make for married life is focusing on a strong walk with the Lord.

The more you follow Him and stay in His Word, you will develop a strong prayer life. You will live a lifestyle of true Christian fellowship. You will become more discerning in selecting a mate. The stronger your prayer life, the stronger your marital relationship will be. When God is truly the foundation of your life, your faith will work itself out in your home and with your spouse. It will overflow naturally. Can two walk together except they are agreed? (Amos 3:3). God was answering my prayers. He also knew I did not want a spiritually immature man, so He led me to pray for him in that area. Allowing me to partner with Him and cause it to come to pass.

Most of the time, we are not waiting on God. But He is waiting on us. You've heard the saying; it is called insanity. Switch up your prayers. You may need to use a different strategy to avoid a delay in your destiny. Do you get it now? So, you pray how you see fit and are led for your future husband. A strong, healthy relationship with the Lord is the basis for a healthy marriage. The Scriptures are clear; love comes only from God, and to love others, we must walk with God and allow His love to flow through us to others. We must remember that love is a by-product of walking in the Spirit. Jesus tells us that Christians are known for their love. True Christianity and love go hand in hand. Love is a choice. Christ looks at us not for what we are but for what we are becoming. Jesus loves us despite us.

Love has always been beautiful to me; being loved makes people feel accepted and valued. He looks at our positive traits and encourages us. Now, I understand why I desired love from people who would never love me the way I deserved. When I began seeking healing, I wasn't being honest with God or myself, ladies.

Looking back, I realize why my King didn't arrive when I wanted him to, which was for a very important reason.

I was called to glorify God, and my marriage would have the same purpose. That simple. All I wanted was one thing, and I couldn't seem to meet a single person that was actually on the same page as me. I thought maybe something was wrong with me. I remember a period in my singleness when I would meet someone I thought was interested in me, and they didn't even ask for my phone number. I see now enormous pressure on women to look "perfect." No wonder many ladies focus on their appearance more than the Word of God. If you spend all your time, energy, and money on how you look while your inner life is a mess, you have your priorities upside-down. It is an issue of the heart. We must understand that scripture does not say that you should not pay attention to your outward appearance. Wearing makeup, fixing your hair, and wearing nice clothing are not wrong. You should look as nice as possible, but your focus should not be on these things. Realize that your beauty begins with your character and radiates outwardly, not the opposite way. On the other hand, when a woman's inner character exemplifies a loving and gentle spirit, it also radiates to her outward appearance.

A godly woman is the most beautiful woman in the world! Your role is vital. You are the missing link in a man's life, and your influence far outweighs anyone or anything else outside of the Lord Himself. Do your attitude and behavior reflect the beauty of a gentle and quiet spirit? "The truth is none of us are easy to date, deal with, or please all the time. We all have vices, attitudes, and ways of doing things that make us who we are. You won't like everything about somebody. It's impossible.

We call this- Life! It isn't about finding the perfect person, and it isn't about living some fairy tale; it's about finding something you're willing to work for, with somebody willing to work with you. That simple. Find someone with a heart for you, and never stop fighting for them. Being in a committed relationship has been a powerful growth experience for me. I understand now that deep relationship is the clearest mirror we have and, therefore, the greatest path to consciousness. However, this is a topic for another book. The right man sacrifices, and the woman submits. He leads, and she follows. He initiates, she affirms. He reflects Jesus, and she reflects Jesus.

To love is to desire, plan, and act for the ultimate good of the beloved. The husband is called to reflect the sacrificial love of Jesus by dying to himself his sin, selfishness, and personal interests and instead enlarging his interests to include his bride's joy in God. Everything God made is good. Everything is for the sake of worship and love. Months passed, and I started praying again about the dream to be certain I heard God say yes. God gave me that dream! I knew what He promised me. I had no earthly idea how it was coming, but I knew I trusted God to do it. At the time, I was in school, in our third class session of Pneumatology: The Study of the Holy Spirit. I never will forget that class! Praise God! It took me a few years to finish that degree. Each week I looked forward to class and said, "Maybe I will get a chance to see him today." May I also add I believe in epiphanies? There is a moment that changes a person. There are many. About six months in 2014, it seemed those moments were all happening in succession. I remember arriving for class one day and having an intense panic attack because my computer wasn't working; *If I don't send this e-mail*. I looked up, and there he was in plain sight. Send.

A False Positive

He was tall and handsome. He had on a nice suit, and his shoes were polished! He smiled as I was leaving my car. He had the prettiest teeth I had ever seen on a man. His cologne was on point too. Not too strong. It was a woody floral musk fragrance with a hint of bergamot and lemon. Sexy scent. I later asked about that cologne. (L'Homme Yves Saint Laurent) I couldn't take my eyes off him as he entered the sanctuary. Class ended as I placed my books in my bag and out of the corner of my eye. I saw him walking towards me, and I looked up. "Here you are? You dropped your pen." He said.

"Thank you, sir!" I said. I smiled.

"You are welcome." He said.

It was "kismet" for me. "I felt an attraction!"

The image of him stayed with me long after class was over. By the end of that year, we started a beautiful friendship. I love the fact that he is thinking about his faith. His relationship with God intrigued me. We could talk for ten hours straight (seriously) and still have so much to say. We were both timid, and it took him a long time to convince me to go with him to a movie. We were inseparable. We complemented each other. We were very comfortable together, and I immediately felt a sense of closeness with Willie. We were finding out things about each other that made us shine. I think there was ease as we talked and communicated. Once our friendship developed, it just blossomed into love. Although, at the time, I was soured on relationships and marriage. Looking back, I think he may have looked at that differently than I did. Because I never assumed that I wouldn't be married again. I wasn't out searching, but I didn't think I wouldn't be. I did respect and love the sort of sense of tradition that Willie stood for, his gravitas, and the way he's a very manly man. That was very attractive to me. I felt like I wanted to do everything I could to respect and honor that, but also to respect and honor myself as a strong independent Black woman. I think that's what confuses men sometimes, but it becomes a balance they eventually find. He indeed treated me nicely. He had every characteristic and spiritual quality I prayed for. I was at peace and confident. I believed that God heard my prayers.

I believed I was worthy of being loved, married, and worthy enough for him. When I first met Willie, I was head over hills. Finally, A Real Man. One who is confident in stamina, status, and satisfied in his Spirituality. He had a lot going for him. He was an intelligent man with good business sense. Not only was he fine, his credentials were impressive, and he was single! And that likely explains why I later became his wife! I could relax in Willie's presence, knowing that this wasn't a man that would break my heart. I trusted him. Yes, I trusted him. Unfortunately, it wasn't in God's timing. For one, we wanted His will and not ours. I was devastated. I cried for a month like rain in a Texas thunderstorm.

Know Your Worth

Most of us strive just to survive singleness and wait to get serious about Jesus and His mission later when things settle down. The work we must do in our hearts and for the sake of the lost is the most important work ever done in history. We've all heard the saying, "If God closes a door, he will open a window," or "if God closes one door, He will open another." Each of us has experienced disappointment in our life.

We feel we are doing what God calls us to do, and BOOM! It gets snatched away, or we hit roadblocks along the way. When an opportunity slips out of our reach, or we face a disappointment in life, God may tell us that it is time to move on and go in a different direction. This one is often the toughest to deal with. We, humans, are funny beings. We think that we have it under control and that we can handle anything. God may close a door at those moments to remind you that He is sovereign. He is in control, not you. He knows how the story will unfold. One evening, I consulted with my spiritual mother. Our conversation was straight biblical. She asked me two questions. "Do you believe God is faithful?" and "Is God not a man that he should lie?" Of course, my response to both questions was "yes." "Now wait on the Lord," she said. And that's what I did. From then on, God began to show me the joy I could have in Him while I waited for a husband. He also revealed some of the lies I believed that kept me trapped in a place of emotional pain and depression after my heart was broken.

Accepting God's love for me had nothing to do with my status. If we are not convinced of God's love before a romantic crisis, we may negatively measure His love for us during or afterward. Our most desperate times of emotional brokenness tend to bring to the surface what we believe about ourselves. His love allowed me time to relax and rest in Him. As a result, He put a new song in my mouth and gave me a heart of gratitude. Wholeness is about embracing our tenderness and vulnerability as it is about developing knowledge and claiming power. I say this because if you put yourself out there and love with your whole heart, you will experience heartbreak. If you're going to try new, innovative things, you're going to fail. If you're going to risk caring and engaging, you're going to experience disappointment. It doesn't matter if a painful breakup causes your hurt or you're struggling with something smaller, like an offhand comment or an argument with an in-law. If you can learn how to feel your way through these experiences and find the peace that faith brings, He will shelter you during life's storms. I always encourage women to give the man a chance-he might be right for them; you just can't see it. Maybe you're longing for friendship or companionship, someone to laugh and cry with. Men do not need to be forced into a commitment.

They will make it very clear when they want it and be very unclear when they do not. Listen to what they say, watch how they behave, and note the signals they send. Never hesitate to take what you think are small things to God; everything is small. I remember a woman who came to me for prayer. She wanted to know if it would be all right if she asked God for two things; if not, she assured me that she would only ask for one. She asked for a husband. Our mission is clear, but we still miss it sometimes. We're so distracted by everything else there is to see and do.

Apostle Paul may have been right about the single person's freedom from anxieties and distractions in marriage. Still, in an iPhone, iPad, or whatever world, we never have trouble finding our share of diversions. The distractions are not (necessarily) burdensome, but they're real. Social media gives us friends and followers, yet our connections are often flimsier than we realize. We can't turn for comfort or help to the "friends" we know only on Facebook. Scattered relationships don't add up to a cohesive society. We get in trouble when we start comparing ourselves to others and think that what they have is better and maybe worth fighting to get. Life is short. We need to stop believing the lie that everything we have here is all we have and start thinking that everything we have here is something to invest in and what's to come. Know Your Worth.

Triggers

After that rocky start, we fell in love and got married. I didn't have to wait long. When my fiancé popped the question, I was thrilled. Less than three months of engagement seemed long enough to prepare for our wedding. Once we set the wedding date, life seemed to speed up, and we couldn't slow it down. My initial ideas about an intimate wedding for our "closest friends and family" quickly succumbed to pressure to hold a blow-out gala in all its Southern goodness. After we posted the news on social media, we were showered with good wishes from friends nearby. Still, I had a lump in my throat that wouldn't go away. For years I knew I wouldn't be able to share this moment with my mother or father, but it was harder than I had expected.

Anytime someone asked when our wedding would be, I would say: "The sooner, the better." I asked my fiancé if we could elope.

He wasn't having that! He didn't even respond. I spent a lot of time reading stories of how motherless brides handled their weddings. All of them said the same; *Memorable Celebrations*.

The loss experience does not have to be the defining moment in our lives. Instead, the defining moment can be our response to the loss. It is not what happens to us that matters so much as what happens in us. Therefore, it is not true that we become less through loss; unless we allow what we lose to make us less. Loss can make us more. It depends on our choices. We've all experienced loss. But that loss doesn't have to define you. Your defining moment can be how you choose to respond to that loss. After a loss, no matter how many years have passed, significant life events are reminders that the person we have lost is not there with us. For our wedding, I had always imagined that my mom would be there for wedding dress shopping and that my dad would walk me down the aisle. The moment became bittersweet.

As my fiancé and I planned our day, we made a concerted effort to include them without making us or any of our guests sad. Because of who my mom was and how she felt about me, I knew she would have wanted our special day to be about Willie and me, not another memorial for her. So we worked hard to find subtle yet meaningful ways to integrate her memory into our day. The bottom of the invitations should read: *"Blessed from above by Robert and Dave Anna."* My brothers would walk me down the aisle to my husband-to-be.

At the reception, I danced with my new father-in-law. And above all, I am grateful that I found a man who loves me like my father loved my mother. I knew I'd shed a few tears on my wedding day. What I didn't do was let those emotions ruin an incredibly special time. Before she died, my mother and I talked about the fact that there would be many difficult and sad moments ahead. But I promised her I would find a way to honor and respect all she gave me in everything that I did. As a tribute to my mother's presence as my "something blue," I had her initials sewn into the lining of my dress in royal blue.

Make It Work

There's a Scripture in the Bible that says, how can two walk together unless they agree? (Amos 3:3). Willie had a process that would lead us into marriage. We went from friendship to fellowship and from fellowship to a relationship. Sometimes we jump straight to the relationship, but we never get to know them individually. So, the friendship is getting to know him and only being friends.

He jokingly admits that when we first met, it was a natural attraction to my outer beauty and later "from the looks to the inner; to my heart." the fellowship was getting to know him spiritually. From fellowship to relationship, now I get to know him on a relationship level, and there's nobody else in the picture.

For me, I think I had to kind of surrender to love. I already felt I loved Willie, but I felt that with the sense of power and independence and all the things I developed as a professional woman over the years. I am still independent, but I also have developed a softness from trying to work through many of the issues I had before our marriage and love him. I had to step back and assess how to pull some of that into my marriage. I had to surrender and embrace our relationship differently.

If you're in a second marriage, you hope you've learned from the first one. Always try to figure things out together. I think the key is finding what works for the other person. You have to know your mate. There was one question I was asked a few times throughout our engagement, "what makes you most anxious about getting married?"

When I asked my god-sister this question, she said, "the hardest thing about marriage was losing your alone time." That stuck with me. Mind you; I possess about 10% of my outgoing, social personality, which worried me, but let me be honest, it terrified me! I'm going from single to a pastor's wife! I decided to answer that recurring question. I was indeed going to lose the time I had to myself. I prayed and wrestled with it throughout our three-month engagement. I knew it would be quite a big adjustment and maybe even a struggle, but God had a plan for my new marriage as He shaped and molded me. Thankfully, I love a good challenge! I created secret forts inside bushes, complete with baby dolls and snacks. I told you growing up; I was considered the token loner kid.

I rode my bicycle up and down the neighborhood streets for hours. I took my dog, Taz, for long walks while singing to myself. If only for a couple of hours, journaling was a regular occurrence to get a reprieve from my brothers. I loved the time alone. As an adult, that did not change. I was the person you felt sorry for in a movie theatre sitting alone. It may seem pathetic, but I was utterly content by myself. Don't get me wrong; I have always had a few friends, and I have a social life, but more than most people, we all need alone time to recharge our batteries.

My Greatest Joy

The days leading up to our wedding were beautiful. With so much joy and memories being created. The excitement to begin a new life with Willie. A prophecy had been spoken over my life for this day where destiny and promise clapped hands. The one I prayed for was the man in my dreams. It hit me all at once. I realized I was in a *Kairos* moment. I bowed before God without caring who was present. A sweet voice whispered, "Elizabeth, this is your moment, your season, and it is for such a time as this." My wedding day was the most incredible day of my life! The peace of God came over me like never before. It felt like I was experiencing sort of an Esther moment. Our pastors performed the ceremony; Dr. Israel Jones, Sr., and Reverend Artist Stringer. Willie and I vowed in front of God and everyone we loved our adoration and lifelong commitment to one another. The reception was full of dancing, toasts, and warm embraces. Our hearts were full. Being one has been the greatest fulfillment in my life!

We are married and love each other more through every obstacle. I am still a newbie in this role as a married woman, but I can honestly say that my favorite time is spent with Willie. I do not crave the solitude I had before marriage. Instead, I find myself craving the quality time with him that I have grown to enjoy. This adjustment to marriage could have been an extremely difficult one. Instead, I long to be with my husband as much as possible! I believe that time is a gift, and it goes by fast. The best way to slow it down is to give moments weight by being fully present, whether by yourself or the ones you love. Although I still like some time to myself, I prefer time spent with my husband and best friend. Two are better!

One thing we do is have one part of our house that we call the common area. Whenever he comes in, and I'm home, I'm in that area waiting on him, and vice versa. We make sure that is our common area. "Now we make it our business that we leave every March for the past five years and go somewhere alone. That is written in stone - that is our time together.

Today, I am so grateful that I trusted God and not man through it all; because Willie truly is my best friend. We can talk about anything. We enjoy listening to what each other has to say. We enjoy each other's company. We add to each other. We certainly laugh a lot together. We are both funny, and laughter brings much-needed levity to our lives. He has a great sense of humor. I think we both bring out the best in each other.

Most importantly, he loves me for who I am, encourages me to do what I like, and supports most of my decisions, even if he doesn't necessarily agree with them. And, of course, I do the same for him. At this point, I am blessed enough to call him my best friend. It's an intimacy we have built and earned over the years. If I had to express my feelings, it would simply be, "Thank you, Jesus" I am thankful to you for exemplifying your love towards me by giving me such a jewel of a man. One who loves me, as Christ loves the church.

ŠËꞓ-ÅþäR̈ꞓ

Ladies, I want to leave you with this thought. "You belong to something big, and that is God! You have a call from God. You cannot allow fear or doubt to keep you from fulfilling it. You are a daughter in God's kingdom. He has called you to lead families to Christ. The King has set you apart to conceive the vision for future generations.

You are born to multiply wherever you are. You are more than just a woman. You are a woman of God created in His image and likeness. Nothing can ever take that identity away from you. Receive the queenly anointing God has bestowed upon all of you whom He has purposed to dream for the nation. You have the right to decide who you want to have dinner with. You don't have to settle for the first person or the person who says you look pretty. You are the one who decides who will share your dreams and laughs at your jokes.

You don't have to settle because you are attracted to them or had a good conversation but did not intend to stay. Don't settle for charm when you know they may not value what you value. Don't settle for convenience without love. Why light a candle when you were taught to love the sun? Especially when you know that love is patient, kind, and not envious. Love is not puffed up. Know your worth! Don't you dare settle for someone who makes you feel less than others? If or when you marry, marry someone who will make you better, challenge you to go deeper with Jesus, and think you're the best thing since his favorite cereal. Pay attention to what your parents, Godly leaders, and prayerful friends have to say. Get them involved from the beginning. Don't wait until emotions are so involved that you can't receive what anyone is saying. Fall crazy in love with Jesus and trust His timing!

We rejoice in our sufferings, knowing that suffering produces endurance, endurance produces character, and character produces hope, and hope does not put us to shame because God's love has been poured into our hearts. (Rom. 5:3–5) So we do not lose heart. God speaks to all of our pain through the Bible. He is the artist who painted all the brightest lights and all the darkest shadows into our lives.

Whatever the future has in store for you, know that Jesus has your best interest in mind. I am overwhelmed by His goodness, His faithfulness, and His hope. I am not only surviving, but I am thriving because my life source is His grace alone. The reality is that all of us can imagine something better for ourselves than our circumstances today. The greater reality is that if you love and follow Jesus, God always writes a better story than you would write for yourself. It's amazing how someone walks into your life one day, and you can't remember how you ever lived without them. "Stay together": "Love one another." And "Stay focused on Christ."

"This Place"

To the man who makes every moment of my life special! Thank you for holding me when I cry and making me laugh. I appreciate you for giving me the shoulder to cry on and being the one I can talk to when my world seems to be crashing and closing in on me. You have proven beyond a shadow of a doubt that I can depend on you. You are selfless. You are the best friend that I ever had. You understand my moods, rants, and irrational thoughts but cherish me irrespective of the oversensitive, stubborn, unbearable me. Thank you for not judging me when I am unnecessarily upset and angry. You calm me down and lift me in my worst times. You encourage me to believe in myself and support me in expanding my interests.

Thank you for taking time out of your busy schedule to spend with me. You listen to and watch chick flicks that I know you would have rather avoided. I walked in love with you with my eyes wide open, choosing to take every step along the way. I have never felt such sincerity and dedication towards a relationship except you. I have never felt so loved and cherished in my entire life. Thank you for making me feel like I'm perfect even though I am not close. Thank you for embracing me for my weirdness and loving me unconditionally. Thank you for apologizing at moments, knowing well that I am at fault. Thank you for not holding anything to your heart and openly communicating your feelings. Thank you for allowing me to love a great Man of God like you. Thank you for covering and protecting me spiritually, emotionally, physically, and financially. Thank you for choosing me, loving me where I am, and telling me I am worth choosing. I love you!" I'm so glad; I'm living in "This Place."

After all, this is what having a best friend is all about. So you can sit at your Table for '2'.

153

CHAPTER 13

Set Apart

*The warrior who fights for the blessings
God has promised and battles to keep the ground
God has granted; stands alert and ready with the
Sword of the Spirit, which is the Word of God.*

Since I made this powerful 91 Psalm declaration, my life has not been the same. My suffering had a purpose: to bring glory to God! Without a prophecy over my life, I do not know where I would be. Bless God! I fought my way back to God. Even now, as I remember, it brings me to tears. For the first time, I could see Him. Sense His presence. I understand He is real. He had created me for a purpose-to bring Him glory. And all that I had endured was to accomplish that end.

God, who knew me and each of us before the foundations of the world, calls us uniquely. Not based on anything we have done but solely on His irresistible grace. And this call often begins with Him answering a simple prayer. Not a theological or learned one, just a sincere cry. Thinking about the days, I wanted to give up! Crying myself to sleep because I didn't know where life was taking me. Am I strong enough to make it to my destination?

Some of you may not believe this, but I'm here to tell you that God has a grand mission with your name on it somewhere. And when you find it, you will say, "This is what I was born to do." God gives His greatest test to His greatest warriors! There is nothing to distract from this Psalm. It was written for everyone in a relationship with God. When you declare the Word of God over your life, you have to walk it out. Before going any further, let me emphasize that Psalm 91 is written to *dwellers*.

It begins with a promise to those who remain, inhabit, and abide in the hiding place or shelter of the most-high God. It promises deliverance and protection not to everyone but to *dwellers*—those who draw daily, habitual strength from their Lord as they sustain an intimacy of fellowship and nearness with Him. They will stay permanently in the shadowing protection of El Shaddai. Don't forget that! We all have "issues" because we all have a story. And no matter how much work you've done on yourself, we all snap back sometimes. So be easy on yourself. God prepares you for the purpose by giving you certain spiritual gifts. Spiritual gifts are special abilities God gives you to do His work in the world. In order to discover God's unique purpose in your life, you must identify your gifts. When you become a Christian, God gives you at least one spiritual gift and usually more than one.

You may not know what yours are or how to use them. You can't learn or earn spiritual gifts by any effort; they're gifts from God. There are Christ-like characteristics that reveal our spiritual maturity. On the other hand, your spiritual gifts reveal your ministry, that is, what God wants you to do specifically to serve Him. All of us are to use our unique spiritual gifts to serve God and others in specific ways in the church and out in the world. No one gift is given to everyone, and no one has all the gifts; that's why we need each other--that's just the way God made us.

Spiritual gifts are not roles or positions in a church. All of us should use our gifts to glorify God. Help others and build up the church. Some of you have the spiritual gift of shepherding and caring for others, but that doesn't mean your calling is to be a pastor. Don't expect *everybody* to have your gifts and to serve and do things the way you do. One of my spiritual gifts is teaching God's Word. I have discovered this through experience and feedback from others. I know I have the spiritual gift of teaching because I am not a natural public speaker. I have always been deathly afraid of getting up and speaking in front of people. I have always had this deep fear of public speaking. I remember having to give an oral book report in my English class. It was required to pass this class which you had to graduate. I worried myself to death over this, but I wisely spent many, many hours preparing for this oral book report.

I wrote a complete manuscript of everything I was going to say, memorized it word for word, and practiced it in its entirety many times. It took a full week for everybody in the class to present their reports, and that week finally arrived. Guess whose name the instructor called to go first? That's right. Yours Truly! It took my breath away; my heart started jumping; my mouth dried up like a desert, but that was okay because I was prepared.

When I got up in front of the class, my mind went completely blank; I couldn't remember the first word I would say. But I had my full manuscript, so I looked down, and my hands were shaking so much that I couldn't read a single word. An awful silence came over the classroom. I was petrified; my heart was pounding; I thought I would pass out.

My teacher came over, put his hand on my shoulder, and said, Elizabeth, "why don't you go sit down, put your paper on your desk, and just read us your report." I did, and that's the only way I got through that embarrassing experience in front of my peers. Thank God my teacher had a compassionate heart! Soon after that, a group of us discussed what we would do after college, and I blurted out, I know one thing. I'll never be a Teacher!

Over the past years, several people have told me that my preaching and teaching have helped them in their personal lives and relationship with God. If what they have said is true, then it has to be a spiritual gift that God has given me because I couldn't do this on my own. I give God the Glory. Determining your spiritual gifts helps you discover what God wants you to do with your life. My most potent spiritual gift is the gift of faith.

Many people find the idea of spiritual gifts confusing, scary, or weird. But the Holy Spirit is not meant to spook us. He is God within us, and His gifts help us to build up each other and the church in supernatural ways. The idea that we have spiritual gifts, and abilities that are not of this world, can be complex for our human minds to grasp. But the Bible helps us understand spiritual gifts, why they exist, and how to use them. The gift of faith enables me to have an *extra* amount of faith that God uses to show His power in ways that will create joy and encouragement for others.

In my profession, I deal with many discouraged people in many discouraging situations: divorced, single, depressed, disabled, and so on. God has given me the capacity to go into almost any problem with a person, no matter how dark or discouraging, and be positive and provide them with encouragement and hope for the future. No, I don't have a degree in this. No one taught me to do this. It is a spiritual gift from God. I will share that trial and error is the best way to discover your spiritual gift. Yes, it will first be in your family, next in the church, and last in your community.

The best way to identify your gift is in ministry. In God's timing, your gift will make room for you. (Proverbs 18:16) You don't want to make your primary way of serving God something for which you are not gifted. Some congregation members don't do their part of the Lord's work that God has called them to do.

I was taught that it puts a drag and drain on the whole church, holding the congregation back from fulfilling its mission. These actions aren't God's will, which brings me to tell you this: Everyone in ministry is not your friend! Stop believing that lie. Can I divulge a time when God took me through a ministry preparation process? A few years ago, I began a mentor/friendship, if you will, with a woman in the church who used the tactics of bullying to chastise me. You may not know what it's like to be anointed and attacked by a minister. You may not know what it's like for another woman or man of God to be a problem to another woman or man of God. The fact that I went to church every Sunday; seeking a closer relationship with God; fellowship with other believers, and becoming a better person. Instead, I was found to be a threat to a - Spiritual Bully.

Bullying is a real problem, and it's demonic. People bully in churches for the same reasons they bully everywhere. Although the situation was new, the feelings of inadequacy felt strangely familiar. Yet this triggered the childhood memories. I am an adult. I was doing my best to recuperate from all past emotional, psychological, physical, social, and spiritual issues in my life. However, something started to change as this particular memory came to light. Wait, I was not to blame for what was happening in her life.

Bullying comes in many forms, including mental, physical, and emotional. It could be as simple as ignoring someone just because everybody else does, posting mean comments about someone online, or sharing a joke at someone else's expense. It's all about control. Bullies typically must have an "enemy" in the church because they aren't happy unless they fight a battle. My presence intimated her! People who are intimidated by you will always try to eliminate you. In my opinion, if an individual is prone to jealousy and is unwilling to admit that they have "negative emotions" or sin like everyone else, they are more likely to bully. Truthfully, we all rightfully look to our church community as a safe place, a retreat into relationships that support, encourage, and challenge us. Whereas, in the family of God, our mission is to come to worship and live a life that is pleasing to God. Together as we work for the mission of the Church to spread the good news of Jesus and welcome sinners. Right!

What happens when we are betrayed by the church people we trust? I'll answer. We become deeply wounded, jaded, and confused, mainly because it goes unchecked. She misunderstood my coming altogether. She lacked spiritual maturity and communication skills as a clergy leader and did not foster a relationship of integrity, truthfulness, or trustworthiness. She thought I was trying to take her place in leadership. My adversary didn't talk directly to me about her complaints. By verbally attacking me in the open at church, she could manipulate leadership and avoid ways to discuss her actions and my concerns. Instead, she gossiped with others about me.

Our words can irreparably hurt the people we should treat with kindness and love. We don't realize that the anger is hurting us too. Think how miserable you feel when you are insulting or cruel to someone. Your body tenses, and your mind feels like it's on fire. You get consumed by your outburst and can't focus on anything else. Anger narrows your world so that all you can see is the insult of the moment. Maybe later, you calm down and go back to apologize, but the harm is already done.

When we react rashly and lash out, it's as if we have shot bullets that can't be put back in the gun. We have to remember that we have the option to react differently. I was walking around angry and upset all of the time. The individual was attacking me unmercifully and untruthfully with accusations that became unbearable. I had about all I could take. Somewhere near the end of that time, I began to shun her during church services and events.

One day at a church event, she made a big show of her actions. She offered a hug, but I dismissed the jester. That is when I realized that I was being bullied, and whatever she had going on with her - it wasn't my fault. I kept trying to find out what was wrong so I could fix it. I tried to get people involved to talk to her about it. Sometimes we think we want to resolve conflicts, but our methods worsen things. Because of pride, some people have gotten too comfortable with disrespecting and mistreating the people of God, and leadership has failed to hold them accountable. People who bully try to protect or gain status and power. It pollutes the body of Christ. All the while, I was right about my intuitions. She had people behind her. In all honesty, the church leadership within the congregation seemed to have supported her bullying.

When I shared the news with a few people, one of them commented, "Really? What happened?" "You should just get over it and move on." Of course, the leadership was assumed to be correct and good under their positions. They didn't address the situation because they were hiding behind things that were going on in their own lives as well. For that matter, there was no policy to bring a complaint or to ask for mediation. Sadly, this was an isolated incident of adulthood bullying. The tension was creating stress and frustration in every area of my life. When experiencing difficult circumstances, we may feel offended if someone suggests that something good can emerge from our adversary.

What the bully did and said to me wasn't about me. It was about her. This individual intended to cause harm from purely personal motivation and the opportunity to do so. My adversary was trying to promote her agenda. People get offended but don't realize they are offending others. They're blind to that fact. We see this all too often. We know the height of narcissism in people. They blame others and don't accept responsibility for their actions. They're not willing to admit their sins. I can see why God used bullying in my life to shape me. I advise you to assert yourself when you are unfairly criticized. Learn about verbal self-defense tactics. Find faithful allies, and don't be silent. Talk to as many people as you will listen about what is happening. You will be tested!

Listen, I don't care how connected you may be to leadership; don't miss talking to the right person, God! We often quickly run into the arms of those in ministry, our family members, and friends for solutions to help us, and we fail to go to Our Father. Before I leave this thought, notice how we can be in the right place with God but connected to the wrong person. Becoming a Christian is a lifelong process of being a disciple and reaching others to make disciples. Whether or not you consider yourself qualified, you have the responsibility and privilege to lead people to Christ for salvation.

Love is the reality that keeps us firmly grounded where we belong, supported by the love of family, friends, fellow Christians, and God Himself. I say this because the single word Love contains the antidote to resolve all the conflicts of bullying and power abuse. Love understands how people are sometimes depleted of self-worth, so they feel the need to dominate and abuse.

The expression being 'in Christ' is shorthand for finding our place among our fellow Christians and in the arms and protection of God himself. Why would we ever need to bully and dominate when we have this reality, the One from which our true identity comes? God's word teaches us not to seek to avenge ourselves but to give a place to God to avenge us. He is our Avenger and Defender. God said, "Vengeance is Mine. I will repay." You can be assured that God is a God of justice, and He's on your side, as long as you don't try to go vigilant on your enemies. He will ensure that they face the consequences of their actions. When you are united with Christ by faith, you are safe. Forever. Not because the rest of your life doesn't matter. However, you can live your life as though other things are more precious than Christ. Our safety rests on God's promise that because of Christ, he will not let us minimize Him without convicting us and causing us again to pursue Him.

In other words, the mark of a Christian is not perfect, as we often stumble and yield to the temptation to put other things ahead of Christ in our affections. We resolve this every day. There is so much more that I could write on this topic of church bullying, which I have not here the space to explore. A whole chapter of Matthew's gospel describes the bullies and abusers of power. I have learned the hard way about the negative impact bullies can have on clergy and congregants. Bullies' control over sound and faithful disciples of Jesus Christ is one of the reasons many churches are unhealthy and diseased. To add insult to injury, nobody addressed the behavior. I thought, "I can endure anything for a short season."

You all better stop BULLYING people! People are hurting!

We need to stop blaming each other for whatever happened, apologize, repent, and do whatever we need to do to get back in the right standing with God so we can stay blessed and protected. As we change our abilities to channel anger, we will see changes in the people around us. Nobody wants to be bullied; we would all rather be understood and appreciated. Letting anger motivate us to correct wrongs has great value, but only when our real goal is to seek a solution and not just prove that we are right.

Use your anger wisely. Let it help you find solutions of love and truth. In truth, we all need restoration. We all need forgiveness and redemption. The realization of our sin allows us to appreciate and acknowledge that others are also on a journey, and we cannot expect everyone to be in the same place in their travels as ours. If we approach people with pre-conceived notions or in judgment, we are not allowing space for the Holy Spirit to use us to work in the lives of those He brings alongside us. "You have heard the law that says, "Love your neighbor and hate your enemy. But I say, love your enemies. (Matthew 5:43-44) Pray for those who persecute you." During those stressful days, a friend asked me how I felt. I told her I was experiencing a "peaceful anxiety." When she looked at me rather quizzically, I explained: "I have had anxiety because I need this woman to leave me alone, and there is nothing I can do about it. But I have great peace because I know I can do nothing about it." Knowing these things are in our Father's hands was comforting. My confidence matched my inability to do anything about the problem in God.

As I prayed about the situation, His grace replaced my anxiety (Philippians 4:6-7). Life's problems can be demanding on us physically, emotionally, and spiritually. Yet, as we learn to trust in the Father's care, we can have the peace that surpasses all understanding and overcomes our anxiety. We can be at rest. And I am! Don't be afraid to speak up. A short time later, I encountered my second public prophetic word aimed at me; of course, I believed it.

This preacher called me out and said, "Young lady in the red blouse at the back of the room, God's going to shift you from where you are, He has prepared you for such a time as this, yes you, and you will begin to teach hundreds of people regularly." "Not me," I thought to myself. I would not remain in a place where I am not welcomed. I had already made up my mind to join a missionary organization in Georgia. I set my mind on spending my time there. I doubted this prophetic word and said, "This cannot be." Then she prophesied by saying, "Even though you say in your heart this very moment, "This can't be, God said immediately." People were clapping and praising God for the word. I was embarrassed. The next week I got to Sunday school early, and the chairman of the deacon board looked at me and said, "I know I haven't asked you, but I have an unusual request for you. The Lord just spoke to me and said," You are supposed to teach our Sunday school once a month." Before I could think about it, I heard myself say yes. I was shocked that I had so quickly agreed with the Lord.

I reluctantly went before the class, and after I finished teaching, the pastor came to the podium to do reflections and asked the class if they wanted me to continue the following month. The same thing happened the next month. The people applauded and were receptive to me, and I began to conclude that God was sending me to teach His Word. We must give space and time for the Holy Spirit to influence and work in the lives of those around us. We should never operate from a platform of judgment and with preconceived notions about people, but instead, live and build relationships in and with the love of Christ. In my opinion, there is a lot of ignorance today concerning spiritual gifts. It manifests in abusing spiritual gifts, ignoring them, neglecting them, confusing them with counterfeits, and overemphasizing the wrong ones. This ignorance has to end. If every one of us were to begin serving in a way God has gifted us, our churches and communities would be transformed; and the Kingdom of God would become a reality here on earth as it is in Heaven. I love the Holy Spirit.

This strange divine emanation reminds us that God is living and breathing in us every moment, every day, with the possibility of changing us, inspiring us, and giving us new life in subtle and not-so-subtle ways. It's a theological way to describe what we often write off as coincidence, synchronicity, or even laughter. You have a God-given gift inside of you that has the power to give direction and purpose to your life and others. It can unlock personal freedom and give you a resounding affirmation of God's value in your life. Why? Because you matter to Him. The Holy Spirit is life, breath, energy, creativity, and power. It is a gentle breeze that relieves our anxiety and calms our fears. My reluctant journey into the gifts of the Spirit was just the beginning. The prophesy I received from the Woman of God saying that I would immediately begin to teach hundreds of people regularly has been fulfilled within a couple of years. I am now teaching Sunday school and bible study under my husband's leadership and pastor, Reverend Willie J. Morgan, Jr.

Most importantly, God has called people to lead and minister to the saved and the unsaved spiritual needs. Yet, they do have their limitations. The experiences of the prophets attest to this reality. Additionally, tragic situations occur in people's lives that are beyond their power to give the comfort that produces inner peace. However, there is one to whom we can turn when confronted with the vicissitudes of life, Jesus, the Word, God's special agent. He possesses the power to heal and restore life. God had a different plan for me that wasn't so strange, but how He communicated this plan challenged my faith. I'm not perfect, but I am forgiven. And I forgive my adversary, for she knew not what she did.

Now, I know those when Jesus Christ hung from the cross. I learned that confidently waiting on God pays off in His established time. Through it all, God sustained me because I stayed silent while doing my part! I'm here to tell you this: whenever God puts a calling on your life, whatever it is, don't ever think for a moment that there will not be distractions. Satan is the master of distractions. He will try to turn you aside from God's words. And if you don't know your calling, you will be easily persuaded. Has it ever occurred to you that God has been watching and protecting you all of your life? This book aims to bring awareness of all the choices that unfurl in front of you during those moments of loss, discomfort, and hurt. God is protecting you. We have all fallen and have skinned knees and bruised hearts to prove it. But guess what! "Nothing can be healed if it stays covered up."

There are many people today who, instead of feeling hurt, are acting out of hurt. Instead of acknowledging the pain they are inflicting hurt on others. Please don't stop being genuine and loyal even if you feel undervalued, unappreciated, or unloved. Don't focus on WHO rejected you because so many are grateful for you. Sometimes the attacks against you aren't because of your actions but rather who you are becoming. There will be a day that God rewards you.

Keep doing what God has called you to do, despite the opposition. Keep trusting God, despite the lack of love and support from the ones you thought would be there. It doesn't matter who left you, who doesn't support you, or who forgot about you, for God will rise and call even total strangers, non-family members, and new people

164

to embrace you, support you, promote you, encourage you, and most of all, love you. God did not remove the mark of hurt from me but rather made it an integral part of who I am. Even though I have suffered, the mark showed me that I am more than a conqueror through Him. A life lived to God's glory is infinitely more valuable. I hope that you have many testimonies of God's power and work in your life. I pray this Psalm to be a prayer in your heart as it is mine, simply because a promise was spoken over my life, and it introduced my purpose through the power of the Holy Spirit. True *dwellers* begin with a state of mind for those of us who are thirsty to see the diacritical mark of being – *Ŝḝt - Ăp̌ăŕⱦ.*

Under the shadow of the Almighty
"in the Secret Place"

There are some things you will only learn from God.

Most people believe God is real, but few people live like it. The result is a widening gap between their theology and their reality. They allow their circumstances to get between them and God instead of letting God get between them and their circumstances. The wisdom and goodness of God have been revealed to me now that I have yielded 'to His inexorable command.' A great many things I had not previously understood are clear to me. Since God has yet to fail me, I have no reason to question His guidance. My only desire is to please Him, not to fight the losing battle of trying to please everyone else.

What do you desire in the time of danger but to abide in the shadow of the Almighty? Make Him your refuge, and He will be your refuge. Dwell in God, and you shall dwell in God. A commitment to a spiritual life requires us to do more than read a good book or go on restful retreats. Jesus often spoke in parables to hide the truth so that only those hungry for God would gain understanding. He said, "I speak to them in parables, because seeing they do not see, and hearing they do not hear, nor do they understand." (Matt. 13:13)

In the same way, the Holy Spirit often speaks to us prophetically in dreams and visions using parables. How can the Holy Spirit speak to us if we do not pause to listen? Quiet time with God, reading His Word, and communicating in prayer are the source of our spiritual life. To be connected through prayer with the living God of the Bible affects your life as nothing else ever can. Eventually, it contributes to your becoming more like Jesus. Yes, God works in us, but He does so through the Holy Spirit, who gives us the wisdom to understand the Holy Scriptures.

The goal is not about our mastering of the Word of God but about the Word of God mastering us, changing our lives and our way of thinking. That is what matters. To be willing to live the truth that we have learned means to submit to that biblical truth. This choice sometimes involves an intense struggle because we are fighting a battle over who will have supremacy in our thinking and life. And, in the end, there are only two sides to pick. When we lead a spirit-filled life, we recognize the power of the Holy Spirit. That is the resurrected force that I believe!

Is it evident I learned about physical and spiritual rejection the hard way? The spirit of rejection was the most brutal spirit I had ever encountered. The religious, educated, knowledgeable leaders of God's people were the very ones who rejected Jesus. You do know that rejection was used as a part of God's divine plan. Scripture says in John 1 verse 11 reminds us that "Jesus came to His own, and those who were His own did not receive Him. For this reason, simply going to church does not satisfy spiritual hunger. The people who knew the messianic prophecies better than anyone else were the ones who should have been first in line to recognize and worship Him.

The ones who called themselves the children of God hardened their hearts against His Son. Yes, the Son of God understands what it feels like to be wounded by cruel rejection. The religious people of His day aimed their verbal missiles at Him, then took decisive action against Him. "Some of the teachers of the law said to themselves, 'This fellow is blaspheming!' The Pharisees said, 'It is by the prince of demons that He drives out demons.' The Pharisees went out and plotted how they might kill Jesus. Then the Pharisees went out and laid plans to trap Him in His words. Then the chief priests and the elders plotted to arrest Jesus in some sly way and kill Him. Those who had arrested Jesus spat in His face and struck Him with their fists. Others slapped Him.

God's people. It saddens me to acknowledge that some of my most painful wounds were inflicted by religious people. They have been considered Christians by themselves and by others. Yet they have been men and women whose words and behavior are inconsistent with what they believe and contradict what God says.

Even now, I shake my head in disbelief as I recall some painful experiences. Listen to me! God is love, and that love is everything. Our true destiny is that love sustains us. Our spirituality gives us the strength to love. You better stop playing with people's lives! Hell is real. If you are going to do anything meaningful with your life, you must develop a strategy for keeping your heart pure.

Here's why: You will be hated by the ignorant because the confidence it takes to win is often misconstrued as arrogance. You will be betrayed by false friends and jealous brothers and sisters because betrayal is the preferred shortcut to success.

You will be used because of the goodness of your heart & your willingness to trust others on credit. You will be misunderstood by the negativity of others who believe you to be a fraud because the only way to prosper (in their minds) is through deceit. You will be co-opted by ambitious people who don't have a creative bone in their bodies. They will use your gift for their gain.

You will be tested by success, failure, sin, and people. You will be celebrated for a season by those who appreciate your efforts, which can give you the false sense that you've arrived. You will be slandered by envious people you encountered along the way who were always up to no good. You will be criticized by those who have never done anything noteworthy. You will be attacked by those who have done what you're doing differently. You will be misrepresented because it's easier for people to do what they want to in your name than to do what you asked them to do. You will be discouraged because things won't always go as planned, and success isn't always as easy as it seems.

You will be forgotten, especially by those you've helped the most because people tend to ask you not to forget them when they're struggling and then forget you after you have helped them. You will sometimes be disappointed because dreams don't always happen on schedule or as planned. You will be successful. And making it to the top of the mountain can be the loneliest thing you've ever experienced. Beloved, don't become insulted or intimidated when Satan's imps don't want you around. You have to learn how to "but" intimidation. If they don't want you around them, don't worry about it. They don't want you around because they see something you don't see in yourself. Your image does not show up in their mirror. They look at you looking for one thing, but when you are traveling with the blessings of God, they don't see you as you are. But GOD!

Despite all the pushing and blockades, God made room for you. What is it entirely to trust ourselves in God's hands? I'm glad you asked, consecrating, devoting, and giving ourselves to His will. We give up ourselves to submit to His disposal and our owner. Yield yourselves unto God, as those alive from the dead, and your members as instruments of righteousness unto God.

How can we trust him until we have given ourselves up to him? Consider what trust is. It is not confidence in particular events but a resigning and committing ourselves to God. Then you will see that His nature relieves much though we have no express promise. Indeed, a mighty God can do all things that we expect from him. He can keep and preserve us when all means fail. The act of faith, *'He that dwelleth'* in the privilege, 'shall abide.' He that doth dwell - shall dwell. That whosoever will trust Himself in God's hands may remain secure under His protection amid all dangers.

A wise God knows what is best for us, and a good God will not forsake his children or people. God is faithful, who will not suffer you to be tempted above that you are able: but will with the temptation also make a way to escape, that ye may be able to bear it; that all things shall work for good (Romans 28). But for disposing of the particular event, on the one hand, God is so wise and good that we need not disquiet ourselves about it. Still, on the other hand, we must not make promises to ourselves nor become false prophets to ourselves nor entertain confidence in particular events without God's express warrant. Build your house with wisdom, understanding, and knowledge. By this, it is established the rooms will be filled with all precious and pleasant riches (Proverbs 24:3-4).

We see none is so wise to guide and direct us as God. So we show that His power is above all power when we can depend on Him. They that cannot depend upon God fly to other means. Some trust in the creature without God. Trust the Lord with all your heart, and lean not to your understanding. In all thy ways acknowledge Him, and He shall direct thy path. (Proverbs 3:5-6)

As in wealth, honor, and favor of men, God is neglected, and the sinner is laid asleep amid the greatest soul dangers. Trust not in uncertain riches. Man being in honor, abide not. How often have we seen the most shining glory go out in a vapor? God can soon lay it in the dust. Yet, living in touch with the Holy Spirit lets us see the light of love in all living things. That light is a resurrecting life force.

From childhood on, I have often reflected on the passage that proclaims: If I speak with tongues of men and angels but have not to love, I am a noisy gong or a clanging cymbal. And if I have the prophetic powers and understand all mysteries and all knowledge, and if I have all faith to remove mountains but have not to love, I am nothing. If I give away all I have, and if I deliver my body to be burned but have not to love, I gain nothing. As I reflect on the obstacles that seemed hard for me, they are no longer obstacles but opportunities, and when I die and stand before my God, I want Him to judge me on how I loved His people and how He allowed me to be in their lives to help them no matter how they treated me. (1 Corinthians 13:1-2).

Believe me when I say this; "I am at peace with myself living in the resurrection of God's love." I know who I am in Christ. I am the righteousness of God. You are too. He is strong and mighty. He keeps no record of sin. Hallelujah! Having walked with Christ since the age of nine, if there is anything that I have learned, we will have circumstances in our lives that we would never choose. I have experienced a lot of pain, but only God could bring me out. God has an appointed time. Choose this day who you will serve. Let God develop you into the strong woman and man He has called you to be. Live a life that counts for His glory. When you give Him the broken pieces of your life, He will keep you in perfect peace. (Isaiah 26:3)

It is my prayer that you will continue to choose well. Please don't envy me. You have no idea how many long nights, early mornings, broke days, empty refrigerators, repossessions, overdrafts, negative account balances, dollar menus, no's, and tears I have seen to get here. God used those things I thought would break me. My pain and tears were for my healing. The valleys of my life have been lonely, but they have borne fruit that the mountains never could.

In an emergency, help is as close as three pushes on the phone. Human rescuers cannot remedy the situations we face often. Many times our crisis requires divine assistance. When that happens, we call a different kind of 911- Psalm 91:1. There, we find the help and protection of our Almighty God.

When we face a life crisis, we often try to survive independently. We forget what we need most; God's protection and the comfort of His presence are always available. Keep God first. Keep your heart pure. Don't become like those who hurt, betrayed, or scared you. Do whatever it takes to make God happy. God is the author of my story, and He is not done writing yet. But, even if today was the last page of my book, it would be a happy ending.

No more apologies. No more uneasiness. This anointing cost me not being the boss of me! There are some things you will *only* learn from God. I conclude my testimony with Psalm 91:1. I treasure my spiritual mother embedded in me as a roadmap: He who dwells in the secret place of the Most High shall abide *Under the Shadow of the Almighty.*

There are some things you will only learn from God.